GADGETOLOGY

GADGETOLOGY

Kitchen Fun with Your Kids, Using 35 Cooking Gadgets for Simple Recipes, Crafts, Games, and Experiments

Pam Abrams

Photographs by Melissa Punch

The Harvard Common Press

Boston, Massachusetts

For Mickey, who made the first meatballs, and
for Jamie, who helped me invent this book

The Harvard Common Press
535 Albany Street
Boston, Massachusetts 02118
www.harvardcommonpress.com

Printed in China
Printed on acid-free paper

Library of Congress Cataloging-in-Publication Data

Abrams, Pam.
  Gadgetology : kitchen fun with your kids, using 35 cooking gadgets for simple recipes, crafts,
games, and experiments / Pam Abrams.
    p. cm.
  Includes index.
  ISBN 1-55832-346-5 (hardcover : alk. paper)
  1. Kitchen utensils—Juvenile literature. 2. Cookery—Juvenile literature. I. Title.
  TX656.A27 2007
  683'.82—dc22

                         2006026172

ISBN-13: 978-1-55832-346-9

Special bulk-order discounts are available on this and other Harvard Common Press books.
Companies and organizations may purchase books for premiums or resale, or may arrange
a custom edition, by contacting the Marketing Director at the address above.

10 9 8 7 6 5 4 3 2 1

Book design by Edward Miller
Photography by Melissa Punch
Food styling by Brian Preston-Campbell
Craft and food prop styling by Laurie Goldrich Wolf

ACKNOWLEDGMENTS

Inventing the recipes and projects wouldn't have been half as fun if I didn't have help.
Thank you to all the kids who helped test and taste, especially Jamie Steiner, Lucy and
Marta Abrams, Miles Matthews, Lily and Theo Giles, Tess Banta, Tessa and Sarah
Barlow-Ochshorn, Bella Schaefer, Charlotte and Henry Ermer, Olivia Wolf, and David
and Hannah Rossler.

A huge thank-you to my creative dream team: photographer Melissa Punch
for her extraordinary vision and talent, Laurie Goldrich Wolf for inspired genius and
immense generosity, and Brian Preston-Campbell, food stylist extraordinaire.

I'm lucky to have friends who cheer me on personally and professionally, especially
Roberta Israeloff, Jenny Bevill, Jeff Giles, Dena Salmon, Elly Silberman, and Michele
Parrella. And thanks, too, to Julie Merberg and the rest of my colleagues at Downtown
Bookworks who make work fun every day.

For support, encouragement, and neighborhood friendship that keeps on giving,
thanks to: Susan Banta, Justine McGovern, Vicki Sher, Kit Warren, Alison Barlow, and
the rest of the mojo moms. Special thanks for special attention to this book go to Ellen
Shea and Emily Waters.

My agent, Rosemary Stimola, got the idea, nurtured it, and found the perfect pub-
lisher. I thank everyone at The Harvard Common Press, especially Valerie Cimino, Bruce
Shaw, and Virginia Downes, for their enthusiasm and dedication, and also the amount
of creative freedom they allowed me. Ed Miller's design was the icing on the cake.

I'm grateful to the following companies: Harold Import, Apple Source, Crate and
Barrel, OXO International, Sur La Table, and Verbena.

Finally, thanks to my loving family: Bob, Mickey, Jamie, Ken, Madeline, Ursula,
Josh, and Debbie. Could we have a little more fun, please? I think not.

CONTENTS

INTRODUCTION

If you're like me, you probably spend a lot of time in your kitchen, whether you're getting a weeknight dinner on the table or because baking a pie on a Sunday afternoon is your idea of pleasure. But does time in the kitchen have to mean precious time away from your children? I've found that the right cooking gizmos and gadgets make it easy to lure kids into the kitchen—to cook with me, to play, or to experiment. If they see me using a rotary beater to whip a bowl of cream, I can guarantee I'll hear, "Oh, can I do that?"

Adults know how to have fun in the kitchen. For children, the fun comes from the beating or whirring or spinning or scooping. Gadgets tap into kids' innate curiosity about pushing a button, turning a crank, or slicing something in half. In this book, you'll find 35 tools—from an apple peeler to a whisk—that lend themselves to fun, each accompanied by inspiration in the form of delicious recipes, ideas for play, and cool experiments.

Crack a bowlful of walnuts with a nutcracker, then use the nuts to bake Fudgy Walnut Brownies and the shells to make miniature sailboats. Think a salad spinner is just for greens? A paper circle and some food coloring can transform this basic kitchen tool into a spin-art machine! Squeeze lemons with a citrus squeezer for delicious homemade lemonade, then use some leftover juice to make "invisible ink."

The 35 gadgets in this book are by no means definitive. New gadgets or variations on classics appear with great regularity these days. Get into the habit of paying attention to what is new on the market and keep in mind how much fun a simple little tool can add to your child's life. Kitchen tools lend themselves, obviously, to food and food preparation. But I hope this book will showcase their versatility . . . for arts and crafts, projects, and for science fun.

Kitchens are the heart of many homes, and those of us with young children practically live in them. Whether you cook often, aspire to cook and need inspiration, or just crave some interactive family fun, this book will provide plenty of ideas. Enjoy!

NOTE ON AGES *The projects in this book are aimed primarily for parents to do with their 4- to 10-year-old children, though there may be instances in which both younger and older kids will happily participate. In most cases, you can easily adapt the specific ideas for your child's age. In some cases, I've indicated that a recipe or activity is particularly suited to a given age group.*

NOTE ON SAFETY *This book is about having fun with kitchen tools—about learning their intended uses as well as discovering new ways to cook and play with them. I encourage kids to experiment with the tools, but that doesn't mean that anything goes! Children should always be supervised when using kitchen gadgets. It's your job to teach them to treat the gadgets with caution and themselves with respect. If you model this kind of behavior and talk with them about where to draw the line, they will grow up to be as comfortable in the kitchen as you are.*

APPLE PEELING MACHINE

Wonderfully old-fashioned and simple, this versatile and fascinating machine suctions to your kitchen counter and has a crank that kids turn manually to peel, core, and slice an apple in one move. Have a lot of apples on hand because once your children are in the groove, they won't want to stop peeling!

Apple Cupcakes with Caramel Frosting

Makes 24 cupcakes

2 ½ cups all-purpose flour
1 cup packed light brown sugar
1 cup granulated sugar
1 ½ teaspoons ground cinnamon
½ teaspoon salt
¼ teaspoon ground cloves
¼ teaspoon ground nutmeg
4 ½ cups apples, peeled, cored, and chopped
½ cup (1 stick) unsalted butter, softened
2 large eggs
¾ cup walnut pieces (optional)
Caramel Frosting (recipe follows)
Novelty toothpicks

1. Preheat the oven to 325°F.
2. In a large bowl, combine the flour, brown sugar, granulated sugar, cinnamon, salt, cloves, and nutmeg. Mix until well blended.

3. Add the apples, butter, and eggs. With an electric mixer, beat on medium-high speed until all the ingredients are well incorporated. Stir in the walnuts, if you are using them.

4. Place 24 cupcake liners in the wells of muffin tins and fill each cup two-thirds full with batter. Bake for 20 to 25 minutes, or until a wooden skewer inserted in the middle comes out clean. Cool completely on baking racks, then frost. Insert fun toothpicks for added charm.

Caramel Frosting

5 1/2 tablespoons unsalted butter
1/3 cup packed dark brown sugar
1/4 teaspoon salt
3 tablespoons milk (or more, as needed)
1 3/4 cups confectioners' sugar (or more, as needed)
1/2 teaspoon vanilla extract

1. In a small, heavy saucepan, melt the butter over medium heat. Add the brown sugar and salt, mixing until the sugar dissolves. Add the milk, turn the heat to high, and bring to a boil.

2. Pour the mixture into the large bowl of an electric mixer and let cool for 15 minutes.

3. Sift the confectioners' sugar into the bowl and beat slowly at first, then on medium-high speed until the frosting reaches a good spreading consistency. Add the vanilla extract and mix again. You may need to add more milk or confectioners' sugar to reach the right consistency.

PLAY
Peel and Play

Set up the peeler at a play date, sleepover, or birthday party. Or bring it into your child's classroom on a day you are visiting. Kids can take turns peeling, slicing, and coring their own apples. Set out shallow bowls of melted chocolate chips, honey, peanut butter, sprinkles, and other favorite toppings. Kids can dip and decorate their apple slices. It's both a treat and a fun activity!

Experiment
One Long Peel

See if you can sustain one continuous peel from a single apple. Guess how many inches long it is, then measure it to see how close you came.

What Else to Do with Lots of Peeled, Cored, Sliced Apples

- **Make a no-bake apple pie.** Put the slices from 4 apples into a microwave-safe bowl. Sprinkle 1 tablespoon light or dark brown sugar, 1 tablespoon butter, ½ teaspoon vanilla extract, and a pinch of cinnamon over the slices. Microwave for about 4 minutes on high power. This quick recipe makes a delicious no-bake dessert, with or without some vanilla ice cream on top.

- **Make sun-dried apples.** Set peeled apple slices (⅛ to ¼ inch thick) on a rack and place it outside in direct sunlight. (Cover it with mosquito netting, available at camping or housewares stores, to keep bugs out.) Bring the rack in overnight and place it outside again in the morning for the next 2 to 3 days, turning the apples occasionally. When dry, place the apple slices in a zipper-lock plastic bag and refrigerate for 2 days. Then place the bag in the freezer for at least 2 days, after which the apples are ready to eat.

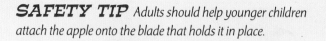

SAFETY TIP *Adults should help younger children attach the apple onto the blade that holds it in place.*

BASTER

Basters are traditionally used to pick up fat and juices from a roasting turkey and distribute them over the bird to brown it nicely. But think about it: A baster essentially sucks something up, moves it, and dumps it out somewhere else. Thus, it creates instant fun for kids.

COOK

Yummy Sparkly Punch

Makes about 2 1/4 quarts

1 quart lemon-lime soda
2 cups orange juice
1 1/2 cups cranberry juice
1 cup apple juice
1/4 cup lemon juice
Ice cubes

In a large plastic pitcher or punch bowl, mix the soda and all of the juices together. Add a lot of ice cubes. Use the baster to transfer punch to glasses.

PLAY
Baster Bash

An easy and fun activity for younger kids is a simple liquid transfer. Set out a baster and two bowls—one empty, one half-full with water or juice. Older kids can race to see how fast they can transfer, or they can mix colored waters together to create new colors, using the baster and clear plastic cups for their experiment. Kids of all ages can float a boat in the bathtub and use a baster to see how much water the boat can take onboard before it sinks.

BOX GRATER

Box graters are the easiest kind of graters for kids to use because they stand firmly on a flat surface. Still, most children will appreciate assistance in holding the grater steady while they work. Cheese, of course, is fun to grate and is the basis for many a child-friendly snack (a bowl of grated cheese, an English muffin pizza, steamed broccoli with melted cheese). But when it comes to grating, don't stop at cheese: The different-size holes on a box grater make interesting crayon rubbings for various art projects. Watch your fingers and have fun!

COOK

Super Easy Lasagna

Serves 6

Nonstick cooking spray for the grater
12 ounces mozzarella cheese, in 1 or 2 chunks
26 ounces store-bought marinara sauce
1 pound no-boil or fresh lasagna noodles
16 ounces ricotta cheese
1/3 cup grated Parmesan cheese

1. Preheat the oven to 375°F.
2. Tape a large piece of parchment or waxed paper onto your kitchen counter. Place the box grater on the paper. Spray the large-holed side of the grater with nonstick cooking spray (this step makes semisoft cheeses easier to grate). Grate the mozzarella.
3. In an 8 x 8-inch or 9 x 9-inch baking pan, spread a layer of marinara sauce. Cover with lasagna noodles, followed by layers of the ricotta, grated mozzarella, and more sauce. Keep layering to fill the pan, ending with a layer of lasagna

PLAY
Wax-Resist Paintings

Lay a box grater down on its side, with any side you wish facing up. Place a piece of heavy white paper on the side that is face-up. Rub the paper with the side of a peeled crayon or oil pastel crayon until a textured pattern appears. Try several sides of the grater for various patterns. Using watercolor paints, paint over the crayon pattern with a contrasting color. (The wax will resist the paint, so the paint will fill in wherever the crayon hasn't colored.) When the painting is dry, cut it into shapes, then glue the shapes onto a piece of heavy white or colored paper to make a collage.

noodles topped with marinara sauce. Sprinkle the Parmesan cheese over the top.

4. Bake for 35 minutes, or according to the lasagna box directions. Let cool for 10 minutes, then serve hot.

What Else to Grate and Eat

- **Carrots,** for a salad or on their own
- **Chocolate blocks,** to sprinkle on a cup of hot cocoa or over ice cream
- **Parmesan or Romano cheese,** for a bowl of noodles or soup
- **Potatoes,** for potato pancakes or hash browns

PLAY
Grater Valentines

Fold pieces of heavy white paper in half to make the cards. Next cut pieces of red and pink tissue paper into heart shapes. Place the hearts over the side of the grater with the smallest holes, and rub gently with oil pastel crayons in contrasting colors. Using rubber cement, glue overlapping tissue hearts to the cover of each card. Let dry, then write valentine messages inside the cards.

PLAY
Grated-Crayon Stained Glass

Peel the paper off whole crayons—the fatter the better. Using the largest holes on the box grater, grate the crayons. Crayons are hard, so it will take a fair amount of elbow grease (or assistance). Sort each color into its own small bowl. Sprinkle the grated crayons in patterns onto the sticky side of a sheet of clear laminating or contact paper. Cover with a second sheet, sticky side down. To melt the grated crayon, use a hot iron. Place the stained glass between a stack of newspapers to protect the ironing board and iron from melted crayon. Iron for 20 seconds, then check to see how the design is coming along. You want the wax to be fully melted but not so hot that it gets liquidy (or it will ooze right out of the laminating paper). Keep ironing, counting, and checking until it looks like stained glass when you hold it up to the light. When the paper is cool enough to handle, cut it into a star, heart, or any shape you like. (A cookie cutter makes a good stencil.) Using transparent tape, hang the stained glass in a window the sun shines through.

SAFETY TIP *Grater blades are very sharp, so teach kids that it is better to sacrifice a stump of crayon or a hunk of cheese than to skin their knuckles.*

CLEANING TIP *To get crayon wax off your grater, pour boiling water over it. If the grater is made of metal, you can melt the wax off by setting it in a pie pan lined with paper towels in a 200°F oven for 15 minutes.*

CHERRY PITTER

Cherries tend to be high on lists of kids' favorite fruits. A cherry pitter is fun to use and has a clear purpose that kids can understand. On one end of this gizmo is a blunt prong; on the other is a little ring that holds the cherry. When you push down, you force the prong through the cherry, pushing the pit out. Pit a few and throw the cherries into pancake batter. Pit a lot, and you can bake a cherry pie. The pitter can also be used for olives—just make sure to wash off the cherry juice first!

COOK

Very Cherry Pudding Cake

Serves 6 to 8

Nonstick cooking spray for the baking dish
3 cups fresh sweet or tart cherries
1 cup sugar (plus ¼ cup more if cherries are tart)
1 cup all-purpose flour
½ cup whole milk
¼ cup (½ stick) unsalted butter, melted
1 large egg
1 ½ teaspoons baking powder
¼ teaspoon salt
Vanilla ice cream or whipped cream (optional)

(continued on next page)

PLAY
Cherry Juice Painting

Dark, sweet cherries have amazing color. When you pit them, juice will accumulate, so do the pitting in a deep bowl to catch the liquid. Transfer the cherries to a colander placed over a second bowl, pressing the cherries if need be with the back of a wooden spoon to extract the juice. Save the cherries for another use. Combine the juices from both bowls. Dip a small paintbrush into the cherry juice and paint a pair of cherries hanging from their stems. You can't get more realistic color! Fold paper in half to make little note cards.

1. Preheat the oven to 350°F. Spray a 1½-quart baking dish with nonstick cooking spray.
2. Pit the cherries using the cherry pitter. Place them in a heavy saucepan with ½ cup of the sugar (and the additional ¼ cup if the cherries are tart). Bring to a boil, then lower the heat, and cook, stirring occasionally, for 10 minutes. Remove from the heat and set aside.
3. In a large mixing bowl, beat together the remaining ½ cup sugar, the flour, milk, melted butter, egg, baking powder, and salt, until well blended. Pour the batter into the baking dish. Top with the cherries (and all their juice). Do not stir! Bake for 45 minutes, or until a toothpick or cake tester inserted in the middle comes out clean. Serve warm or cold, with ice cream or whipped cream if desired.

What Else to Do with Lots of Pitted Cherries

- **Make ice cream:** Prepare cherry-vanilla ice cream, either from scratch or by mixing the cherries into store-bought vanilla ice cream.
- **Freeze them:** Mix the cherries with sugar and pack them into plastic freezer containers (use ¼ cup sugar for every 2 cups cherries). When you need a bit of summer, thaw some for cherry pancakes, pie, crumble, or whatever you wish.
- **Blend a smoothie:** Mix a handful with plain or vanilla yogurt, honey, milk, and ice for a fresh cherry smoothie.

What to Do with Lots of Pitted Olives

- **Slice them** up to top a homemade pizza.
- **Sprinkle them** into a salad or a pasta sauce.
- **Stuff them** with whipped cream cheese (use a toothpick) or an almond half, or skewer them, alternating with small cherry tomatoes.

CITRUS SQUEEZER

Calling all strong kids! It's time for you to press down superhard and turn, turn, turn! That's the name of the game if you're using an old-fashioned tabletop squeezer, also called a juicer. These days you can find big fancy press squeezers, electric juicers, and all kinds of hold-in-your-hand gadgets. Any of them will work to extract juice for food or fun. For the lemonade recipe that follows, send the kids to the produce section to count out the 20 lemons you'll need.

20-Lemon Lemonade

Makes 1 gallon

³/₄ cup sugar
¹/₂ cup water
20 lemons
Ice cubes

1. Place the sugar and water in a small saucepan. Bring to a boil, stirring until the sugar dissolves. Set aside to cool.

2. Slice each lemon in half. Squeeze the juice out of all the lemons. Remove the seeds by pouring the juice through a strainer. (Save the juiced halves to play one of the games suggested.)

3. In a large pitcher, combine half the sugar water and half the lemon juice. Add enough cold water to fill the pitcher about three-fourths of the way full. Stir well and taste. Is it too sour? Add more sugar water. Is it too sweet? Add more water. Is it not lemony enough? You know what to do. Experiment until the lemonade tastes just right. Add ice cubes to fill the rest of the pitcher.

For More Fun

If you have any leftover lemon juice and sugar water, mix them together and pour the mixture into ice cube trays. The frozen cubes of concentrate can be melted later on and mixed with water or seltzer for a quick lemonade refresher.

PLAY
Lemon Lineup

As you're making lemonade (or squeezing lemons for any other reason), line up the lemon halves, cut side down, on a clean counter. After you've squeezed a lemon half, put it back in the line. Every once in a while, guess which halves have been squeezed. Mix them up and guess again. Older kids like getting points for correct guesses, so invent a system—perhaps one point for every correct guess, minus one point for each incorrect guess. The game ends when all the halves have been squeezed. Add up your points!

> **GADGET TIP** *Roll and press whole lemons across your counter before cutting them in half, or microwave them for 20 to 30 seconds. Either method releases some of the juices for easier juicing (doing both releases even more juice). Squeezing is hard work, so take turns with your kids. Or while you do the juicing, let them play Lemon Basketball.*

PLAY
Lemon Basketball

Place a trash bin (without the lid) or large, deep plastic bowl in an open area of your kitchen floor. As each lemon half is squeezed, let your child throw it into the container from a predetermined distance. Two points for every basket!

Experiment
Invisible Ink

Squeeze the juice from several lemons and pour it into a shallow bowl. Using a small paintbrush, draw a picture or write a secret message on heavy white paper. (You won't be able to see the lemon juice after it dries.) To reveal the hidden words or pictures, hold the paper over a light bulb until the words appear.

COOKIE CUTTERS

There are few greater pleasures than baking cookies with kids, and the fun is greatly enhanced when you use cookie cutters. I like to think of projects involving rolled cookie dough as more of a decorating activity than a baking activity. The multistep process is long for most kids—making the dough, letting it chill, rolling, baking, and cooling—all before you get to the really fun part: decorating! I do as much as I can up front, then call the kids when I'm ready to ice and decorate.

The key to great-looking decorated cookies is to use royal icing. Older kids can pipe the icing through a pastry bag to outline the shape, which makes the cookie look neat. And kids of all ages (and pretty much all adults) have a blast decorating with colored sugars, sprinkles, little candies, paint-on color, and other decorations.

Cookie cutters are available in virtually any shape you can imagine. When my son Jamie was studying U.S. geography at school, he was assigned a report on Texas. So we ordered a Texas-shaped cookie cutter from Omaha-based Kitchen Collectables (see Resource Guide, page 87) and made cookies for the class. Lucky for his classmates he didn't get Rhode Island!

Perfectly Iced Cookies

For the Royal Icing (makes about 2 cups)

3 ³/₄ cups confectioners' sugar, sifted (or more, as needed)
3 tablespoons meringue powder (available at baking supply stores)
2 tablespoons warm water (or more, as needed)
¹/₂ teaspoon vanilla extract
Food coloring (optional)

4 to 5 dozen sugar cookies, made from Roll-Out Cookies (page 67) or store-bought sugar cookie dough

Colored sugar, sprinkles, decorating gel or icing, and/or light corn syrup (optional)

1. In a large bowl using an electric mixer, combine all the icing ingredients and beat on high speed for 5 minutes, until you have a consistency like that of heavy cream. Adjust the consistency if needed by adding more sugar or water, 1 teaspoon at a time. Refrigerate until ready to use. Bring back to room temperature and stir to achieve the same consistency.
2. Divide the icing into small bowls and add food coloring if desired. The icing technique will depend on your child's age and patience level. Here are some options:

- **The youngest kids** can spread the icing onto the cookies with the back of a teaspoon or a clean paintbrush dipped in water, then decorate with sugars, sprinkles, or candies while the icing is still wet.
- **Older kids** can hold a cookie by its edges and dip one side directly into the bowl of icing. Then they should flip the cookie right side up and place it on a rack to dry. They can add decorations to wet cookies or let dry and then create designs with store-bought gel decorators, colored icing from a squeeze bottle, or diluted food coloring applied with a paintbrush.
- **Very dexterous kids** can spoon icing (with a thicker consistency) into a small plastic squeeze bottle (available at craft or baking supply stores), then outline the cookie with icing and let dry. They can then fill in the middle with the same colored icing (in a thinner consistency) using the back of a teaspoon and a paintbrush and let dry. Finally, they can decorate by painting letters or designs on the cookie with a clean paintbrush dipped in warmed light corn syrup, then sprinkle the corn syrup with colored sugars or sprinkles. Or pipe designs onto the cookie using the thicker icing.

Cookie Ideas
- Use alphabet cookie cutters and bake your child's name.
- Use a hand-shaped cookie cutter and give it a cool manicure.
- Have a bake sale to raise money for a cause, using appropriate cookie cutters: peace symbols, whales, donkeys, or elephants.

Eggs-in-Bread

Serves 2

2 slices sandwich bread
Nonstick cooking spray, butter,
    or vegetable oil for the pan
2 large eggs

1. Place the bread slices on a cutting board
   and, using a cookie cutter, cut out a shape—
   any size is fine as long as the bread still
   has a solid frame.
2. Set a frying pan or griddle over medium
   heat and spray with nonstick cooking spray
   or coat with butter or vegetable oil. Fry the
   bread for 30 seconds.
3. Using a wide spatula, carefully flip the bread
   over. Crack each egg directly into the hole
   in the bread slice and cook for about 2 $\frac{1}{2}$
   minutes, until the eggs set. (Fry the cutouts,
   too, to serve on the side.)
4. Transfer to a plate. Kids often like to break
   the yolk by pressing a fork down right in
   the middle of the hole. Yum!

PLAY

Cookie Cutter Mobile

Use cookie cutters in the shapes of a crescent moon, multisize stars, and a variety of circles (for planets) to trace shapes onto cardboard or balsa wood. Cut out the shapes and paint them on both sides with neon-colored paints. When dry, push a small hole in the top of each shape with a tapestry needle. Thread neon-colored lanyard string through each shape. Hang the shapes from a painted dowel rod. Tie two lengths of lanyard string to the ends of the rod and then tie them at the top. Hang and admire. Or attach your neon universe to the underside of the dining room table. Throw a blanket over the table and go in with a flashlight to view the pretend night sky.

CORER

A corer is a refreshingly simple gadget that offers kids many ways to explore cylinders and circles. It is designed to remove the cores of fruit such as apples and pears in one tubular shape. And it is terrific for that purpose. But don't stop there. You can also cut small holes out of cucumber rounds, sliced tomatoes, cheese, bread, and more. Or try using the corer to create "tubes" of edible apple, perfect for stacking, dipping, and even building a log cabin.

COOK

Circle Snacks

Serves 4

1 medium-size cucumber (about 8 inches long)
About sixteen ½-inch-thick slices of your favorite cheese
About 16 saltine crackers

1. Peel the cucumber and slice it into ½-inch-thick rounds. Using the corer, remove the middle of each slice.
2. Place the slices of cheese on a cutting board. Using the corer, cut out rounds of cheese and fit them into the holes in the cucumber slices. Place each filled cucumber slice on a cracker. Arrange on a plate and serve.

PLAY
Edible Log Cabin

Core an apple and discard the core. Then push the corer through the rest of the apple lengthwise to make logs. You'll get 4 or 5 logs out of a large apple. Trim the ends off the logs to even them out, and slice each one in half lengthwise, Lincoln Log–style. Your logs will have a flat bottom side and a rounded top side. Lay 4 logs, flat side down, in a square. Build the cabin up, using peanut butter as your mortar (it may help to pat the apples dry). Make a chimney out of raisins (cut in half—or use currants) cemented with peanut butter. Try not to eat until your cabin is complete!

Experiment
Holes

What else can a corer core? A quarter loaf of bread? A tomato? A hard-boiled egg? Look for foods with a pliable texture. To make sure that the gadget will go in one end of the food and come out the other, measure its length and find foods that are at least 2 inches shorter than the corer.

For More Fun

Corers cut perfect circles, and enough perfect circles make polka dots! Try this: Punch holes out of a fried egg, a red pepper, and whole-wheat toast, and have a plate of polka dots for breakfast.

EGG SLICER

For a fun snack or as part of a meal, give your child a hard-boiled egg served with an egg slicer. The simple act of bringing the parallel blades down on a springy peeled egg and turning it from a perfect whole to perfect slices seems almost magical. There are some other fun uses for this gadget, too, as you will see.

Cubist Egg and Cheese Salad

Serves 2

2 to 4 hard-boiled eggs, cooled and peeled
One 8-ounce chunk mozzarella cheese
1 cup shredded or torn lettuce (optional)
¼ cup of your favorite salad dressing (optional)

1. Put each egg in the slicer lengthwise and slice. Carefully lift it out and turn it 180 degrees, setting it back down in the slicer. Slice again crosswise, and your egg will be perfectly cubed.
2. Repeat this slicing and cubing process with the mozzarella cheese.
3. Sprinkle the cubed egg and cheese over a plate of the greens (or not) and drizzle with the dressing (or not). Or keep the cubist motif going and serve ingredients in "squares" on a plate. Some kids like the egg yolks and whites separated. Serve right away.

PLAY

Play Dough Pictures

Roll colored Play-Doh or Easy Homemade Play Clay (page 60) into egg shapes. Place the dough in the egg slicer and slice. You will have ovals to use as the base for a face or balloon. Press in features—use colored clay, beads, seeds, sequins, buttons, hardware such as nuts and bolts, steel wool and cotton balls for hair, and so on.

PLAY (AND EAT)

Edible Funny Faces

Roll homemade or store-bought biscuit dough into egg shapes. Place the dough in the egg slicer and slice. You will have puffy round faces. Place on ungreased cookie sheets. Press in edible facial features: currants, raisins, sunflower seeds, poppy seeds, ground cinnamon, nuts. Brush on red food coloring for rosy cheeks. Bake in a 450°F oven for 8 minutes, or according to package directions. Let cool—and then devour!

For More Fun

Even very young children love to crack hard-boiled eggs, and there's very little that can go wrong. Older kids find it fairly hysterical to crack them against their foreheads. Whatever method you choose for the initial crack, using water will help remove the rest of the shell easily.

FLOUR SIFTER

A sifter is one of the first tools of the baking process that kids can use. One reason children like operating a sifter is because they stay in complete control: The flour comes through the sieve only when they squeeze the handle or turn the crank. Plus, sifting makes a neat sound.

COOK

Crisscross Gingerbread Cake

Makes one 8-inch square cake

1¼ cups all-purpose flour
1½ teaspoons ground ginger
1 teaspoon baking soda
½ teaspoon salt
½ cup granulated sugar
¼ cup (½ stick) unsalted butter, softened
⅓ cup molasses
⅓ cup boiling water
1 large egg
⅓ cup confectioners' sugar
Whipped cream (optional)

1. Preheat the oven to 350°F. Grease an 8-inch square baking pan.
2. Sift the flour into a large bowl. Gently stir in the ginger, baking soda, and salt. Set aside.
3. In another large bowl, cream the sugar and butter together until smooth. Add the molasses, water, and egg, and beat until well incorporated. Mix the dry ingredients into the wet ingredients and mix until just blended. Pour into the prepared pan. Bake for 30 minutes, or until a toothpick or cake tester inserted in the middle comes out clean.

4. Cool in the pan for 10 minutes, then invert to remove, and finish cooling the cake on a wire rack.
5. Cut 8 thin strips of paper toweling, each about ½ inch wide by 10 inches long. Crisscross the strips over the cake in a woven pattern. Sift the confectioners' sugar all over the cake. Gently lift the paper off to reveal the design. Serve the cake with whipped cream on the side, if desired.

PLAY
Buried Treasure Mountains

Sifters make flour come out in nice, neat mounds, which makes them ideal for creating these "mountains." On a clean kitchen counter or plate, sift 1 cup of flour. Carefully place a small, lightweight object on top of the flour (a plastic cake topper, a cut-up drinking straw, or a corn chip, for example). Sift another cup of flour directly over the object until it is completely hidden and your mountain is bigger. Repeat the process two or three times, but leave the other mountains empty. Invite a friend to guess which one has the buried treasure. To test for treasure, you can poke a bamboo skewer though the mountain, dig up the mountain with a teaspoon, or press your palm onto the mountaintop and push right down to the bottom. Try making mountains out of flours of various colors and textures, such as wheat, corn, or rye flour.

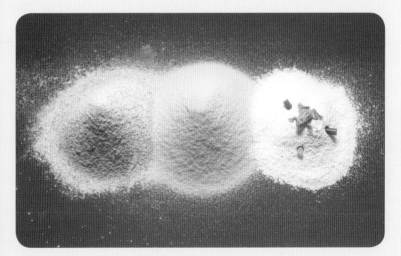

FOOD MILL

Food mills come in many sizes and price ranges. Manual baby-food mills are fun for making mush for little ones; fancy countertop mills sport large-handled cranks, food slides, and "waste" tubes. What they all have in common is the magic of turning a crank and watching foods transform: Tomatoes become sauce, chickpeas turn to hummus . . . you can imagine the intrigue.

COOK

The World's Simplest Pasta with Fresh Tomato Sauce

Serves 4 to 5

4 pounds very ripe tomatoes
3 tablespoons olive oil
Salt and pepper to taste
1 pound pasta in your favorite shape
Grated Parmesan or Romano cheese for sprinkling

1. Cut the tomatoes into quarters and transfer them to the mill. Turn the crank and watch the seeds and peel separate from the pulp. Discard the seeds and peel, and toss the crushed tomatoes in a large serving bowl with the olive oil, salt, and pepper.
2. Cook the pasta according to the package directions. Toss with the fresh tomato sauce, sprinkle cheese over the top, and dinner's ready!

Other Food Mill Ideas

- **Applesauce:** Quarter a few apples and cook them until soft in a small covered pot with an inch of water. Don't bother to peel or core the apples—the food mill will separate the pure fruit from the waste. Once pureed, add cinnamon, as you wish.
- **Hummus:** Drain a 15-ounce can of chickpeas and put them through a food mill. To the mashed chickpeas, add 2 tablespoons olive oil, ½ cup tahini, 2 cloves crushed garlic, 1 tablespoon lemon juice, and salt to taste.

PLAY
Taste Test

What makes something have a taste? With this experiment you'll realize that it takes more than just your tongue!

Using a food mill, puree cooked carrots, then cooked lima beans, and then a cooked potato. Place each food in its own small bowl. Blindfold a couple of friends, have them hold their noses, and give them a small taste of each puree. Can they taste which is which? The tongue can only tell what is sweet, salty, sour, and bitter. The nose adds much more distinguishing detail through aroma. Take away the nose, and most mush tastes like . . . well, mush!

FUNNEL

No matter your age, there is something supremely satisfying about using a funnel to transfer matter from one place to another. For children, there is also curiosity and pleasure as they watch a big quantity of something flow through a small tube. Funnels naturally invite investigation and experimentation. I have never met a kid who isn't delighted by the sight of a sink or bathtub full of water and assorted funnels. In fact, I have taken to making a birthday gift for three- to eight-year-olds of a big, colorful pail filled with a half-dozen funnels in different colors and sizes and a small plastic pitcher. It's always a major hit. Look for brightly colored soft funnels made of silicone; they're easy to manipulate and clean.

COOK

Cinnamon Toast

Serves 1, 2 . . . or a crowd

3/4 cup sugar
2 tablespoons ground cinnamon
White or whole-wheat bread
Unsalted butter

1. In a small bowl, combine the sugar and cinnamon until well blended. Place a small funnel in the top of a clean spice jar and pour the sugar mixture into the jar. (This mixture will keep indefinitely.)
2. Preheat the broiler. In a toaster, toast the bread slices (as many as you want to eat) until crispy, then butter each slice. Liberally sprinkle the cinnamon sugar onto the slices and broil until the butter begins to bubble and the sugar looks melted.

PLAY
Funnel Fun

• If weather permits, it's great to let kids play outside with water and funnels. Set up a large plastic bowl filled with water and an assortment of nonbreakable cups, nesting bowls, pitchers, ladles, scoops, or anything else that will transfer water into the funnel. If you have an outdoor pool, throw a bunch of funnels in for extra water play.
• Set your child up at the kitchen sink with assorted funnels, plastic cups, and bowls. Just add water and let playtime begin. This is often a good diversion while you're preparing dinner nearby. Try stacking all the funnels one on top of the other and watching the water flow through all of them.
• Funnels are especially fun in the bathtub when combined with a few good pouring tools. Hair washing can be a little less painful if you use a funnel to wet and rinse your child's head (it's easy to aim the water away from the eyes). And children will eagerly rinse off soapy bodies if they can do it with a funnel.

Funnel Cakes

Makes 6 to 8 funnel cakes

3 large eggs
2 cups whole or 2 percent milk (or more, as needed)
$1/4$ cup granulated sugar
$3 1/2$ cups all-purpose flour (or more, as needed)
2 teaspoons baking powder
$1/2$ teaspoon salt
Vegetable oil for deep-frying
Confectioners' sugar for sprinkling

1. In a large mixing bowl, beat the eggs. Add the milk and granulated sugar and beat until combined.
2. In another large bowl, sift the flour with the baking powder and salt. Slowly add the dry ingredients to the wet, stirring between additions and mixing until the batter is smooth. The batter should be thin enough to pour though a funnel with an opening of $1/2$ inch. Add more flour or milk as necessary to achieve the right consistency.
3. Pour the vegetable oil into a heavy, straight-sided 8-inch frying pan until it reaches a depth of about 1 inch. Heat over high heat until an instant-read thermometer registers 375°F. Put your finger over the small hole of the funnel and add about $3/4$ cup of batter. Holding the funnel over the hot oil, remove your finger and carefully pour the batter into the center of the pan, gradually spiraling outward in a circular motion. Cook the funnel cake until golden, 2 to 3 minutes. Turn the cake with a pair of spring-loaded tongs and cook on the other side until golden, about 1 minute. Remove and drain on paper towels.
4. Sprinkle or sift confectioners' sugar over the top and serve right away.

Experiment
Funnel Magic

Before your "performance," secretly dip a cotton swab into food coloring and swab the inside tube of a funnel. Set the funnel over a clear glass. Repeat with two other colors so that you have three clear glasses set out on a counter with funnels inserted in them. Then, using a pitcher filled with plain water (let your audience see that the water is pure), invite a guest to fill the three glasses with water—each of which will turn its own magical color!

GARLIC PRESS

The garlic press crushes and extracts juice from garlic cloves. Despite its strong flavor, garlic is an ingredient in a surprising number of foods that kids like, including garlic bread and pickles. In addition to garlic cloves, you can also press biscuit dough through a garlic press to make "strands" that are good for building edible baked nests. A garlic press is a good tool for a would-be superhero: With sheer strength you can squeeze two handles of steel together and reduce a solid to itty-bitty mush.

Pickles!

Makes 6 pickles

4 cloves garlic
$^3/_4$ cup white vinegar
$^1/_3$ cup salt (Kosher salt or rock salt works best)
2 tablespoons pickling spice
2 sprigs fresh dill
6 Kirby cucumbers

1. Peel the garlic and, using the garlic press, crush the cloves into a large plastic container for which you have a tight-fitting lid. (The container should be able to hold 64 ounces of liquid.) Add the vinegar, salt, pickling spice, and dill, and stir well.

2. Wash the cucumbers, but do not peel or cut them. Place them in the container and cover them completely with water. Cover the container with the lid and refrigerate. The cucumbers will be half-sour pickles in 2 weeks! After they turn into pickles, you may store them in glass jars in the refrigerator for up to 3 weeks.

PLAY

Jelly Bean Nests

Press small bits of store-bought refrigerated biscuit dough through a clean garlic press. Open the press and keep adding dough and pressing to make long strands. When you have strands about 6 inches long, cut them from the press and gently shape them into little nests right on an ungreased baking sheet. Bake according to the package directions. When completely cooled, fill with jelly beans.

For More Fun

• Press sugar cookie dough through a clean garlic press to form "spaghetti" cookies. Press the dough right onto a prepared cookie sheet and bake in a 350°F oven until golden.

• You can transform Play-Doh into lovely strands of hair for a clay face by pushing it through a garlic press. (See the recipe for Easy Homemade Play Clay on page 60.) If you stack a few colors in the garlic press, you will get beautiful multicolored strands. Kids especially like this activity because it seems like magic to produce a single thread that blends from, say, blue to pink to green.

GADGET GUIDANCE *Buy a garlic stripper—a little gizmo that makes peeling garlic a snap. It's a good companion gadget to use with a garlic press. The best ones for kids are made of rubber and resemble a thin piece of hosing. Place a clove of garlic inside the hose, apply pressure, and roll. The garlic will slip right out of its skin.*

A handheld potato ricer looks like a big garlic press, and in fact it can be used for the activities with clay or cookie dough. The strands will be thicker, but that's okay. In fact, some children find it easier to push contents through a ricer.

CLEANING TIP *Clean a garlic press by poking a toothpick through its holes. Eliminate the garlic smell from your hands by rubbing them with half a lemon.*

HAND BLENDER

The handheld electric or battery-operated immersion blender wasn't designed just for kids, but it might as well have been. They can make their own smoothies in minutes, watching the ingredients blend and froth before their eyes. Most cooked vegetables can be pureed with this gadget; blend in some broth and add leftover pasta and you've got soup for supper. Cleanup is also easy, as this gadget is nice and small. Cordless, battery-operated hand blenders are the easiest for kids to operate by themselves.

Cuisinart
SmartStick
EXTENDABLE SHAFT

COOK

Bananafana Smoothie

Serves 1

1 banana
1/4 cup milk
1/4 cup plain or vanilla yogurt
1 tablespoon orange juice

Put all the ingredients into a tall, sturdy plastic glass. Using a handheld blender, blend until the banana is crushed and the drink is thick and frothy. Serve right away.

PLAY (AND DRINK)
Rainbow Milk

Using a hand blender, combine 6 ounces milk with ¼ teaspoon vanilla extract, 2 teaspoons sugar, and a few drops of food coloring in your favorite color. It's fun to serve this drink to a crowd, giving children different colors of the rainbow.

PLAY (AND EAT)
Liquid Watermelon

Cut watermelon into chunks and remove the seeds. Place the chunks in a deep bowl. Press the hand blender down into the melon and puree. Four cups of watermelon chunks will yield 2 ½ cups of pureed watermelon. Once you have watermelon puree, here are three yummy things you can make with it.

· **Happy Watermelon Soup:** Pour the watermelon puree into a shallow soup bowl. Make a face, using honeydew balls for the eyes, a blueberry or blackberry for the nose, and a swirl of sour cream or vanilla yogurt for the mouth.

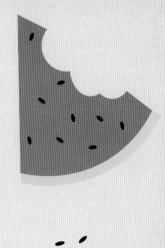

· **Mini Melon Pops:** Pour the puree into ice cube trays, cover with plastic, and poke toothpicks through the plastic into each section. When frozen (after about 6 hours), remove the plastic, and your mini pops are ready to eat.
· **Sweet Red Fizzy:** Fill a tall glass with ice cubes. Fill the glass three-quarters full with watermelon puree. Fill the glass the rest of the way with club soda or 7UP. Add a sprig of spearmint and serve with a straw.

KITCHEN SCALE

There are three kinds of kitchen scales: balance, spring, and digital. Most cooks today use one of the latter two varieties. Easy science lessons come when children use a scale to compare weights, measure out ounces and pounds, and estimate how much something will weigh. A kitchen scale will easily bring out your child's natural curiosity.

Countdown Trail Mix

Makes about 5 cups

10 ounces raw or roasted cashews
9 ounces dried golden raisins
8 ounces salted or unsalted sunflower seeds
7 ounces dried cranberries
6 ounces salted or unsalted roasted peanuts
5 ounces mini chocolate chips
4 ounces dried apricots, chopped if desired
3 ounces mini pretzels
2 ounces yogurt- or chocolate-covered raisins
1 ounce dried cherries

After weighing each ingredient, pour it into a big bowl. Toss the mixture together with clean hands or a large wooden spoon. Store the trail mix in an airtight plastic container or individual zipper-lock plastic bags. Take it to school for snacks or on hikes or long car rides.

Experiment
The Great Flour Test

Professional bakers often like to use scales rather than measuring cups because they get a more precise measurement. Try this: Measure 1 cup flour in a dry measuring cup. It should weigh about 125 grams (or 8 ounces). Pour it into the bowl of a scale and see how accurate the measurement is. Then try it again, starting with a new cup of flour. You'll see that every time a cup of flour is measured, it is a bit more or a bit less than 125 grams. Some of the factors that affect weight are whether the flour has been sifted, if it was poured or scooped, and how tightly it is packed. When a cup of flour is weighed on a scale, you can add or take away flour until the scale registers 125 grams. It's a great lesson in precision.

PLAY
Which Weighs More?

Gather a bunch of household items: a candy bar, a saltshaker, a potato, a cell phone, a jar of pennies, a box of pasta, a book, a set of keys, and so on. Set the kitchen scale to zero. Take turns guessing which of two items weighs more: a potato or a cell phone? A jar of pennies or a set of keys? The person who asks the question is allowed to hold the items, but the guesser must try to determine only by looking. Keep score by giving one point for each correct answer.

MARINADE INJECTOR

When it comes to shots, most kids would prefer to give than to receive. A marinade injector not only makes this possible, but it also makes it tasty. This gizmo looks like a giant needle and is traditionally used to inject liquid flavorings into meat. For kids, though, cooking or playing with a marinade injector is the ultimate sweet revenge.

COOK

Flavor Changers

Cranberry, apple, mango, or grape juice
A bowl of strawberries
1 large orange, unpeeled

Pour the juice of your choice into a cup and fill the injector one-fourth to one-half full. Inject the juice slowly into the strawberries, one at a time. Taste a strawberry. Try other juice flavors, continuing to taste the strawberries until you have found a combination that you like best. Fill the injector again with the juice of your choice, one-fourth to one-half full, and puncture the orange right through the skin, injecting the juice slowly, so that the liquid doesn't squirt back out. Slice and serve.

Experiment
Guess That Flavor

Play a guessing game using flavored extracts such as peppermint, lemon, vanilla, and almond. Without anyone seeing, in a small bowl, dilute ¼ teaspoon extract with 2 tablespoons hot water. Stir in ½ teaspoon sugar until it dissolves. Inject the flavoring into a strawberry, a piece of plain cake, or even a glass of water. Ask a friend to guess the flavor.

PLAY
Color Shooters

Fill a tall, clear glass three-fourths full with water and place it on a counter. In a measuring cup, mix about 10 drops of food coloring with ⅛ cup water. Fill the marinade injector with the colored water. Submerge the needle into the clear glass of water and shoot for a magnificent blast of color! (Note: The less diluted the food coloring, the more intense your blast will look.)

What Else to Do with a Marinade Injector
• **Shoot water** into your open mouth.
• **Squirt melted butter** into a baked potato.
• **Set up a target outside,** fill the injector with water, and see how far away you can stand and still hit a bull's-eye.

MEAT POUNDER

What kid wouldn't want to use a heavy, solid disk to smash something? That is the simple allure of the meat pounder. Think of it as a smasher, be careful, and you'll have a ton of fun.

GADGET GUIDANCE *For art or cooking projects, use heavy cardboard or a stack of newspapers for padding the counter or table before pounding.*

COOK

Kid-Friendly Chicken Satay

Serves 4

1 pound skinless, boneless chicken breasts
1 cup unsweetened coconut milk
2 cloves garlic, minced
1 tablespoon freshly grated ginger or 1 teaspoon
     ground ginger
1 tablespoon dark brown sugar
1 tablespoon soy sauce
1 tablespoon sesame oil
1 tablespoon lime juice
Store-bought peanut sauce (optional)
15 or so bamboo skewers

1. Cut the chicken into strips, about 3 inches by 1 inch. Place them between 2 sheets of waxed paper. Pound the chicken with the meat pounder until the strips are very thin.
2. Combine the coconut milk, garlic, ginger, brown sugar, soy sauce, sesame oil, and lime juice in a large bowl. Add the chicken, toss to coat well, cover, and let marinate in the refrigerator for at least 2 hours, or up to overnight.

3. Preheat the oven to 375°F or preheat a gas or charcoal grill. Soak the bamboo skewers in water for at least 30 minutes.

4. Thread each piece of chicken onto a skewer, loosely folding each piece in half and piercing through the folded meat to form a loose gather. Arrange the skewers on a baking sheet and bake for 10 to 15 minutes, or grill over medium heat for 8 to 10 minutes, turning once halfway through the cooking time. Serve warm, with peanut sauce if desired.

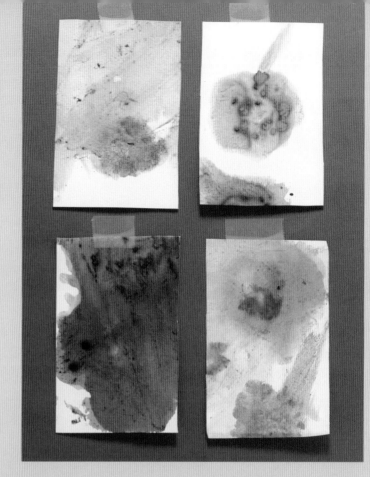

PLAY
Smashed Berry Prints

Gather berries from bushes or from your local produce department or farmers' market—the deeper the color, the better. Place the berries on half of a piece of white watercolor paper, a thick white paper towel, or other absorbent paper. Fold the other paper half lightly over the berries. Smash, unfold, and examine your print. Pick berry seeds out with a pair of tweezers, if necessary.

MELON BALLER

This handy little scooper makes irresistible, perfectly round balls of melon. Kids like both making and eating melon balls with equal enthusiasm. To get well-rounded scoops, push the melon baller deep into the melon and twist it, focusing on your wrist action. Have extra fruit on hand to practice with, as kids get better at this technique with time. Because melon ballers are crafted with a small draining hole in the spoon, they are fun to use with ink or paint for art projects, too.

Watermelon Basket

Serves 16 to 20

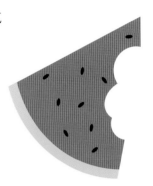

1 cantaloupe
1 honeydew melon
1 pint *blueberries*
1 watermelon

1. Cut the cantaloupe and honeydew melon in half and scoop out and discard the seeds. Scoop out rounds of fruit with the melon baller and place in a large bowl. Add the *blueberries* and toss very gently.
2. To make the *basket*, slice a small, thin piece off the less attractive side of the watermelon so that it sits flat on a work surface. With the tip of the *knife*, score the watermelon in half horizontally. Mark a vertical strip about 2 inches wide in the middle of the watermelon; it will form the handle of your *basket*. Cut around the melon following the lines you've made and carefully separate the cut sides from the body of the watermelon.

SAFETY TIP *Quarter the melon balls if you're serving them to children under four, as their round shape makes them a choking hazard.*

3. Using the melon *baller*, hollow out the inside of the watermelon. Add the watermelon *balls* to the rest of the fruit in the bowl. After removing all the *edible* parts, take a large spoon and gently scrape out the insides of the watermelon *basket* to make it smooth. Fill with tossed fruit and set out for people to serve themselves. Note: Don't try to lift the basket by the handle!

PLAY
Dribble and Splat Paintings

Lay down a piece of watercolor paper. Hold your finger over the hole in the melon baller (on the underside of the scooper). Carefully pour diluted colored ink or food coloring into the spoon (or use an eyedropper) and hold it over the paper. Remove your finger. Move the melon baller in different directions as the ink dribbles and splats onto the paper. When the ink dries, finish the painting. Let the ink spots serve as your starting point. Is there a body that needs a head? A head that needs a body? A flower that needs petals and a stem? Just as it's fun to look at clouds, it's fun to look at dried ink spots and swirls and see the possibilities.

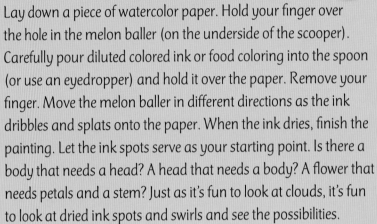

Quiz: Which is the mortar and which is the pestle? This cooking tool is about as low-tech as they come, but that doesn't detract from its kid appeal: You get to smoosh something or grind it into a paste or powder using your own strength. Using this tool makes you feel as if you'd fit right in in ancient Egypt. It also brings out great flavor, making it popular with adult cooks, too. Mortars and pestles come in a variety of sizes; if you have a small one, you may need to work in batches.

Green Bean-Sesame Sauce Toss

Serves 4 to 6

4 tablespoons white sesame seeds
1 tablespoon soy sauce
1 tablespoon rice vinegar
1 teaspoon sugar
1 pound fresh or frozen green beans, cooked
   and cooled

1. Pour the sesame seeds into a dry frying pan and roast over high heat until they start to pop, turn color, and give off a nutty aroma, 3 to 5 minutes. Allow to cool, then put the sesame seeds in the mortar and grind them with the pestle. Push hard! (You may need to do this task in 2 batches.) When the seeds resemble a rough paste, transfer them to a small mixing bowl or cup. It's fine if there are some whole seeds left.

2. Stir in the soy sauce, rice vinegar, and sugar, and mix well. Toss the sauce with the green beans and serve right away.

What Else to Do with a Mortar and Pestle

- **Crush peppermint candies** to sprinkle over vanilla or chocolate ice cream.
- **Having trouble swallowing a pill?** Grind it into a powder and mix it into a glass of juice.
- **Make your own peanut butter:** Use 1 teaspoon vegetable oil for every ⅓ cup peanuts and grind until chunky or smooth, according to your preference.
- **Spice up your pizza!** Put 1 tablespoon dried oregano, ½ teaspoon coarse salt, 2 peppercorns, and, if you like it really spicy, 1 hot dried chile pepper into the mortar and pestle and pound into a powder. Sprinkle over homemade or store-bought pizza to jazz it up.

PLAY

Homemade Sidewalk Chalk

Wash and gently dry the shells from 6 eggs. Peel away the "skin" that sticks to the inside of the shells and discard. Grind the shells, in batches, into a fine powder with the mortar and pestle. Depending on your child's strength and patience, you may have to finish the job. In a small bowl, mix 1 teaspoon hot water with 1 teaspoon flour until smooth. Add the eggshell powder and, if you want colored chalk, ⅛ teaspoon powdered tempera paint. Combine. With your hands, form the mixture into a stick of chalk. Wrap it in a paper towel and leave it on the counter. Let the wrapped chalk harden and dry, which takes about 3 days. Go outside and draw!

NESTING BOWLS

Kids love bowls that fit inside one another for lots of reasons: They can sort them by size, stack them, put stuff in them, turn them over and hide things under them. Grownups love them because nesting makes for easy storage. They're very versatile, and they allow you to set up ingredients in advance, making it easier for kids to skip the prep work and help you really cook or bake.

COOK

Tacos Your Way

Makes 8 tacos

1 pound ground beef
1 package taco seasoning
Shredded cheese for garnish
Shredded lettuce for garnish
Cubed tomatoes for garnish
Sliced olives for garnish
Sour cream for garnish (optional)
Guacamole for garnish (optional)
Sliced or chopped jalapeño peppers
    for garnish (optional)
8 taco shells

1. Cook the beef with the taco seasoning according to the taco package directions.
2. Put each garnish ingredient in one of the nesting bowls. Everyone can build his or her taco with the different garnishes, according to individual taste.

PLAY
Keep the Change

All you need for this great math game is a jar of change (or your purse) and four little nesting bowls. Ask your child to sort the change by pennies, nickels, dimes, and quarters, putting quarters in the littlest bowl and pennies in the biggest one. Older kids will enjoy the added challenge of totaling up the money (especially fun when they're learning to use a calculator). Estimate the amount in each bowl before doing the actual addition.

PLAY
Sort for Mom

Set five empty nesting bowls out on a table. Set up a plate of five different ingredients, such as uncooked pasta, raisins, baby carrots, dried beans, pretzels, and the like, and have your child sort the foods into the bowls by type. This is an especially good side-by-side activity in the kitchen: You cook dinner while your child sorts ingredients.

NUTCRACKER

Sometimes I buy nuts in the shell because I know that if I set them out with a nutcracker, anyone who passes by will start cracking. It can put you into a Zen-like state—not a bad thing, but be ready for a big store of nutmeats. If they don't inspire immediate baking, they will freeze well in zipper-lock plastic bags. As for the shells, save them for craft projects and games. Older kids like the challenge of cracking perfect halves. The relatively soft shells of almonds make that variety the easiest for little kids to crack. Nutcrackers are also fun to collect—there are hundreds of types and designs.

Fudgy Walnut Brownies

Makes 24 brownies

20 to 30 walnuts in the shell
4 ounces unsweetened chocolate
1 cup (2 sticks) unsalted butter
1 ³/₄ cups sugar
4 large eggs
1 teaspoon vanilla extract
1 cup all-purpose flour
¹/₄ teaspoon salt

1. Preheat the oven to 350°F. Grease and lightly flour an 11 x 9-inch baking pan.
2. Crack enough walnuts to measure 1 ¹/₂ cups. Break the walnuts into pieces and spread them out in a single layer on a baking sheet. Toast for 8 minutes, giving the sheet a shake once or twice for even toasting. Remove from the oven and set aside to cool.
3. Place the chocolate on a cutting board and chop finely with a sharp knife. (It is surprisingly easy to chop chocolate, making it a step that older kids can try with supervision.)
4. Melt the butter in a medium-size saucepan over low heat. Remove from the heat and add the chopped chocolate to the pan. Count to 60, saying "Mississippi" to space the intervals.
5. Whisk the butter and chocolate together until smooth. With a spatula, transfer the mixture to a large mixing bowl and allow to cool for 8 minutes.
6. Whisk in the sugar until blended. Add the eggs, 1 at a time, and whisk until well incorporated. Whisk in the vanilla extract. Add the flour and salt and stir with a wooden spoon until you have a smooth batter. Stir in the toasted walnuts. Spread the batter evenly into the prepared baking pan and bake for 25 minutes, until the edges of the brownies begin to pull away from the sides of the pan. Cool for 20 minutes on a wire rack before cutting and serving.

PLAY
Walnut Shell Sailboats

Crack a few walnuts until you have some perfect halves (try applying light pressure). Hot-glue the head of a matchstick inside the middle of each shell and let dry. If you don't have a hot-glue gun, you can use Elmer's glue or clay. Cut triangular sails out of decorative oilcloth, paper, or waxed cardboard (from a milk container, for example). Glue the sail to the matchstick, and your little boat is ready to launch. It's fun to blow a fleet of boats across the bathtub with a straw!

PLAY
Almond Heads

An almond's oval shape and relatively smooth surface make it perfect for faces. Crack a bunch of almonds, working to get as close to perfect shell halves as you can. Draw faces on the outside of each shell with a felt-tip marker (dark-colored indelible ink works best). Add hair or hats made from *Easy Homemade Play Clay* (page 60), yarn and doll's accessories, or Play-Doh. Sink the "neck" into clay to display. A whole row of faces looks great on a mantel!

What Else to Do with Cracked Nut Shells

- **Make shakers:** Put the shells into an empty, cleaned frozen juice can. Seal the ends with masking tape. Wind two shades of colored masking tape all around the container. These shakers are great fun for younger kids.
- **Use them in collages:** They make real-looking tree trunks.
- **Create a funky frame:** Scatter them onto a picture frame and cover with decoupage medium, such as Mod Podge.
- **Play a shell game:** Hide a dried bean or small piece of uncooked pasta under three perfect walnut halves, rearrange the halves, and guess which one holds the surprise.
- **Play word games:** Write letters on large pieces of shell, à la Scrabble tiles. Put them all in a bag and shake them up. Each person gets seven letters and tries to make words. For children learning to spell, give them the letters of a particular word (their name?) and invite them to arrange the letters into that word.

PASTA SPOON

Pasta spoons are sometimes called pasta forks, and they truly are a combination: long-handled scooper-stirrers with tines. They can be made of wood, nylon, or stainless steel and come in a variety of designs. What they have in common is that all make stirring, sampling, and serving spaghetti, fettuccine, or linguine fun and easy. The tines also offer creative possibilities with yarn or colored rubber bands.

Fettuccine Alfredo with Peas

Serves 6

1 pound fettuccine
½ cup (1 stick) unsalted butter
2 cups heavy cream
1 teaspoon salt
1 cup grated Parmesan cheese
1 cup peas, cooked

1. Cook the pasta according to the package directions.
2. Melt the butter in a large saucepan over medium heat; add the cream and salt. Raise the heat and bring to a boil, then turn the heat down and simmer for 3 to 5 minutes, until the sauce begins to thicken.
3. Remove the pan from the heat and add the cooked fettuccine, Parmesan cheese, and cooked peas. Toss with the pasta spoon to combine and serve right out of the pot.

Pasta Spoon Puppets

These homemade toys are great for puppet shows. Use strands of colored yarn or curling ribbon for hair, attaching it to a pasta spoon with wire or glue. Add facial features: stick-on scrapbooking charms, beads, or rhinestones. Adorn with party favor–sized hats.

Experiment
Spoonful of Strands

Lift a spoonful of cooked pasta strands out of a bowl. Hold it up high and estimate how many strands you have. (Hint: half as many as you can see.) Next, mix a little oil into a bowlful of cooked spaghetti, using the pasta spoon to coat evenly. Can you form letters of the alphabet from the strands? Feel free to cut them up if that helps.

PASTRY BAG

Pastry bags are great for piping everything from delicate icing to the filling for deviled eggs. Decorating tips, which fit inside the bag, are available in all kinds of shapes and sizes. You can pipe out squiggles, roses, and flat and tubular lines in a multitude of widths. Before filling a pastry bag, fold the bag down about 2 inches to form a cuff. Fill the bag, unfold the cuff, and twist closed. Younger children can keep the top twisted closed with a rubber band or bag clip.

Deviled Eggs

Makes 8 deviled eggs

1 tablespoon white vinegar
4 large eggs
2 tablespoons mayonnaise
$1/2$ teaspoon Dijon mustard
$1/4$ teaspoon salt
2 teaspoons minced fresh Italian parsley (optional)
Paprika for garnish (optional)

1. Bring a medium-size saucepan of water to a boil. Add the vinegar, which will prevent the eggs from cracking. Turn the heat down to low.

(continued on next page)

2. With a slotted spoon, gently lower the eggs, one by one, into the simmering water. Simmer for 12 minutes. Drain and cool in a bowl of cold water.

3. Drain and refrigerate the eggs for at least 1 hour or up to overnight.

4. Peel the eggs and cut each one in half lengthwise. Gently remove the yolks and place them in a food processor or small bowl. Add the mayonnaise, mustard, salt, and parsley, if desired, to the yolks and process or mash together until smooth. Using a spatula, place the yolk mixture in a pastry bag fitted with a plain or fancy tip. Pipe the filling into the egg-white halves, swirling upward as you go.

5. Sprinkle with paprika, if desired. Cover and refrigerate until ready to serve.

Other Foods to Stuff

- Fill cooked large pasta shells with ricotta cheese.
- Fill ready-made cannoli shells with a mixture of 2 cups ricotta cheese, ½ cup confectioners' sugar, ¼ teaspoon vanilla extract, ¼ teaspoon ground cinnamon, and ¼ cup mini chocolate chips.
- Fill a scooped-out cupcake with whipped cream (and sprinkles!).

PLAY
Piping Play Dough

This oily dough passes through the pastry bag easily. Use as many different tips as you have for a variety of designs. Mix 1 cup light-colored oil (such as canola) with 6 cups flour in a large bowl with a wooden spoon. Turn the dough out onto a counter and knead until thoroughly blended. Divide the dough into sections and color each with food coloring. (Add a bit more flour if the dough is *too* oily.) Fill the pastry bag and pipe out designs into a shallow container, such as a cigar box or shoebox top. Try putting two colors on top of each other in the bag to create a pretty multicolored coil.

BUYING TIP *Single-use pastry bags, sold in packs of 20 or so, are good for kids, as they can have several bags going at once—and cleanup is a snap.*

TIP TIPS *Ateco, a cake-decorating supply company, makes a fantastic selection of tips that you can purchase in sets or separately, at cooking stores or at wilton.com (see Resource Guide, page 87). Keep in mind that tips are tiny and tend to get lost in kitchen drawers. Store them in a see-through plastic container along with your pastry bags, which will fold up nicely into a small package.*

PASTRY BLENDER

Pastry blenders are used to cut fat into flour without warming the dough (as hand kneading does). If you can keep the dough cool when you're making something like a pie crust, it will come out tender and flaky rather than tough. Kids like using a pastry blender because they can slowly watch the ingredients transform themselves into dough. Many recipes call for flour and shortening to be combined until it resembles "little peas," a challenge kids can understand. It's also a tool that requires a lot of physical energy.

Brown Sugar Pie

Makes one 9-inch pie

FOR THE CRUST
1 cup all-purpose flour
1/2 teaspoon salt
5 tablespoons unsalted butter, chilled
3 to 4 tablespoons ice water

FOR THE FILLING
1/2 cup (1 stick) unsalted butter, softened
1 cup packed light brown sugar
3 large eggs
1 cup buttermilk
1/2 teaspoon salt
1/2 teaspoon ground cinnamon
1/2 teaspoon ground nutmeg
1/2 teaspoon finely grated lemon zest

(continued on next page)

1. To make the crust, sift the flour and salt together into a large mixing bowl. Cut the butter into pieces and add it to the bowl. Combine the butter and flour mixture with a pastry blender, lifting it up and down and moving it back and forth through the dough until the dough resembles little peas. Sprinkle 3 tablespoons of the water over the dough and blend again, until it forms a solid ball. Add the remaining 1 tablespoon water if the dough seems too crumbly.

2. Wrap the dough well in plastic, press it into a disk, and refrigerate for at least 1 hour.

3. Preheat the oven to 375°F.

4. Using a floured rolling pin, roll out the pie dough on a lightly floured surface and press it into a 9-inch pie pan. Cover the dough with aluminum foil and pour in about 1 1/2 cups of dried beans or uncooked rice to weigh it down. Bake the crust for 8 minutes. Remove the weights and foil and prick the bottom of the shell all over with a fork. Return the crust to the oven and bake for 8 more minutes. Remove from the oven and reduce the temperature to 325°F.

5. To make the filling, cream the butter and brown sugar together in a large bowl with an electric beater until fluffy, about 3 minutes. Add the eggs to the butter mixture and beat until just combined.

Pour in the buttermilk and add the salt, cinnamon, nutmeg, and lemon zest. Beat until just combined.

6. Add the filling to the partially baked pie shell and bake until the custard is set and golden brown, 55 to 65 minutes. Cool on a wire rack and slice to serve.

PLAY

Basket Weaving

Use a rolling pin to roll several colors of Play-Doh or Easy Home-made Play Clay (page 60) out onto a board in a square shape. The square should be at least 8 inches and approximately ½ inch thick. Push one outer end of the pastry blender into one edge of the Play-Doh. Gently rock the tool all the way down and around to make strips that are 8 inches long. Push the strips through the wires of the blender to separate them. Next, cut out a solid dough circle with an 8-inch circumference (the length of the strips). Break 3 wooden bamboo skewers in half and push the 6 broken ends into the circle, around the edges. Weave the dough strips in and out of the skewers to build a basket and add a handle if you wish.

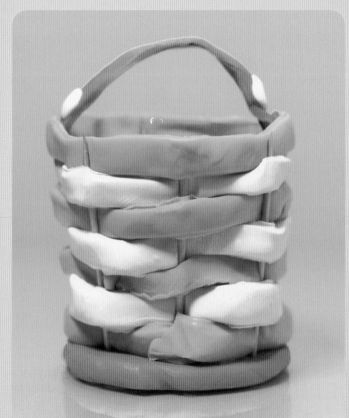

What Else to Do with a Pastry Blender

- **Rock the pastry blender** back and forth in different directions on a thick sheet of white paper (construction paper works well), pressing down to make indentations. Gently rub the paper all over with the side of a crayon. These pastry blender rubbings come out different every time you make them!
- **Make "not quite mashed" potatoes** by cutting up boiled spuds with the pastry blender. When cooked potatoes are cool enough to handle, slice them into rounds, place each round flat on a cutting board, and let kids slice and dice them every which way with the pastry blender.
- **Lay the tool flat** on a piece of paper and use the tines to outline a smile. Fill in the face freehand.
- **Bake biscuits!** Find a recipe for savory biscuits online or in a favorite cookbook. Pastry blenders make perfect dough for hot-from-the-oven biscuits.

PASTRY CUTTER

A pastry cutter is like a small pizza wheel, but without the sharp blade. The scalloped edges on its wheel make a decorative pattern in the pastry, which kids find neat. Pastry cutters were invented to cut dough, or to close up the sides of foods that have filling on the inside and dough on the outside, like pie crusts, dumplings, and ravioli. Whether you roll a pastry cutter over pie dough or Easy Homemade Play Clay (page 60), you're bound to have a lot of fun.

Lattice Strip Apple Pie-and-a-Half

Makes one 9-inch and one 4-inch pie

FOR THE CRUST

4 1/2 cups all-purpose flour

2 teaspoons salt

1 1/2 cups (3 sticks) unsalted butter or solid vegetable shortening, chilled

12 to 15 tablespoons ice water

FOR THE FILLING

10 to 12 large apples

1/3 cup sugar

Juice of 1 large lemon

1 1/2 teaspoons ground cinnamon

3 tablespoons unsalted butter

1. To make the crust, sift the flour and salt together into a large bowl. Cut the butter into pieces and add it to the bowl. Combine the butter and flour mixture with a pastry blender until it resembles little peas. Sprinkle

58

12 tablespoons of the water over the dough and use a wooden spoon to bring the dough together with a few quick strokes. Add more water if the dough seems too crumbly. Knead the dough a few times and shape it into 2 balls, one using two-thirds of the dough and the other using the remaining one-third.

2. Divide both balls in 2 pieces, one a little larger than the other, and wrap each in plastic. Press all 4 balls into individual disks. You and your child will each have enough to make a bottom crust and lattice strips for the top of your pies. Refrigerate for at least 20 minutes.

3. To make the filling, peel, core, and slice the apples into eighths. Place in a large bowl and toss with the sugar, lemon juice, and cinnamon.

4. Preheat the oven to 350°F. Remove the dough from the refrigerator and let it sit at room temperature for 10 minutes.

5. Set out a 9-inch and a 4-inch pie pan. Take the 2 larger dough pieces and roll them out with a floured rolling pin on a lightly floured surface. Roll from the middle outward in every direction until each circle is 1 to 2 inches wider than its pie pan. Carefully fold the dough in half, and then in half again. Gently lift them off the board and set them in the pie pans, unfolding so that the dough hangs evenly over the sides. Refrigerate for 20 minutes.

6. Meanwhile, roll out the 2 smaller disks until they are

¼ inch thick. Using a pastry cutter, cut the dough into long strips about 1½ inches wide for the large pie, and about ¾ inch wide for the small pie.

7. Spoon the filling into the chilled pie crusts and dot the top with the butter. Create a lattice top on your pies by overlapping the strips and trimming the ends if necessary. Tuck the ends of the strips into the inside edges of the pie shell, pressing to seal tightly. Fold the bottom crust up and over the rim and crimp with a pastry cutter. Bake the small pie for about 40 minutes and the large pie for 1 hour, until the top pastry is browned and the filling is bubbling. Cool on a rack for at least 30 minutes before serving.

PLAY
Easy Homemade Play Clay

Here's a great recipe for basic clay. Serve it up with a pastry cutter, and your child will take it from there. The possibilities for rolling and cutting are endless. Put 1 cup flour, ½ cup salt, 1 cup water, ½ teaspoon cream of tartar, and 1 teaspoon vegetable oil into a large saucepan. Cook, stirring constantly, over medium heat until the dough forms a ball. Turn the clay out onto a floured, disposable cutting board (or one you don't mind staining with color). When the clay is cool enough to handle, knead it until smooth. Divide into smaller balls, and knead different shades of food coloring into each. (Gel-based colors add terrific vibrancy to this clay, but any kind of food coloring will work.) The clay will keep, stored in airtight plastic containers in a cool dry place, for several months.

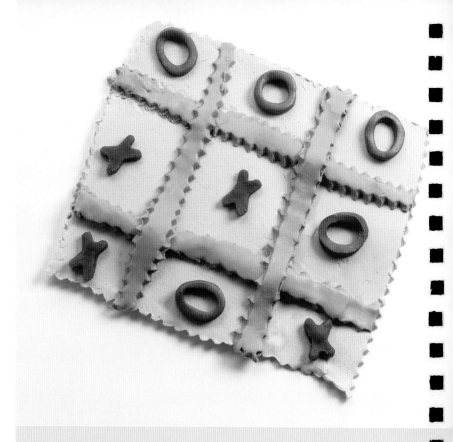

PLAY
Tic-Tac-Dough

Roll a ball of Easy Homemade Play Clay out with a rolling pin. Cut a tic-tac-toe board with a pastry cutter and play. For the X's and O's, cut more clay with the cutter, or use small alphabet cookie cutters. When the game is over, gather up all the dough and roll it out for another round.

PEELER

Mastering the peeler makes kids feel grown up. They've probably seen you peel thousands of potatoes, carrots, and apples in their lives so far. Carrots, parsnips, and other straight-edged produce are easier to peel than round ones, so start with those. When learning to peel, kids often hesitate to press down hard enough as they draw the blade against the vegetable. Encourage them to "press and peel" simultaneously while you hold the food steady.

COOK

Sweeter Sweet Potatoes

Serves 6

2 pounds sweet potatoes or yams
2 tablespoons vegetable oil
1/4 cup dried cranberries
2 tablespoons dark brown sugar
1 teaspoon ground cinnamon

(continued on next page)

1. Preheat the oven to 375°F.
2. Peel the potatoes and cut them into 1-inch cubes. Toss the potatoes and vegetable oil in a casserole dish that will hold the vegetables in a single layer. Cover with aluminum foil and bake for 20 minutes.
3. Remove from the oven and stir. Mix in the cranberries, brown sugar, and cinnamon. Return the casserole to the oven, uncovered, and bake for another 30 to 40 minutes, until the potatoes are nicely browned.

PLAY
Crayon-Peel Frame

Cut out two 5 x 7-inch pieces of cardboard, and then cut a 4 x 6-inch window out of one of the pieces. Cut a small triangular "hook" from a third piece of cardboard and slip one end between the first two pieces. Glue the top, bottom, and one side of the window to the whole piece of cardboard, reinforcing the hook with tape on the back of the frame. Set the frame on top of several sheets of clean, white paper (photocopy paper is perfect). Brush rubber cement or craft glue onto one side of the frame. Using the peeler, scrape curls of crayon directly onto the wet glue. Use lots of crayons in a variety of colors until you have a nice, thick layer. The crayon peels will be delicate, so the less you touch them the better. As you work, gather up the peels that have accumulated on the paper and, making the paper into a cone, pour them directly onto the frame. Continue applying glue and peeling, in sections, until the frame is completely coated in crayon. Let dry. Slip a 4 x 6-inch photo into the open end of the frame and display.

COOK

Carrot Peel Salad

Serves 4

¹/₃ cup raisins
4 to 6 large carrots (the fatter, the better)
1¹/₂ heads iceberg lettuce
3 tablespoons canola oil
1 tablespoon lemon juice

1. Soak the raisins in a cup of hot water for 20 minutes.
2. Peel, rinse, and dry the carrots. Set aside.
3. Cut or tear the lettuce and add it to a large salad bowl. Peel the carrots into strips right into the salad bowl. You can hold the carrot against the side of the bowl to press down firmly and peel. (Hint: The less you push down, the thinner the strips will be. Play with variations.)
4. Drain the raisins and add them to the salad bowl.
5. Mix the canola oil and lemon juice together in a cup, pour over the salad, and toss well.

PLAY

Art and Architecture

Peel a carrot, a potato, a red apple, and a green pear. The multicolored strips can be used to "weave" or make designs on a counter- or tabletop. These works of art won't keep, but they're fun for kids to play with while you're working in the kitchen on something else. Your child can also play young architect and lay out square or rectangle "rooms" from the peels. Inhabit with dollhouse furniture, little plastic people, or action figures.

BUYING TIP *Most peelers are made for righties or the ambidextrous. If your child is left-handed, try the Kuhn Rikon Single Blade Swiss Peeler (available at thegadgetsource.com; see Resource Guide, page 87). Its ergonomic design works for both righties and lefties.*

POTATO MASHER

It's hard to find a kid—actually a person of any age—who doesn't like mashed potatoes, and this tool makes that dish easy and fun to prepare. But a masher is good for more than just spuds. Try mashing hard-boiled eggs for egg salad or ripe bananas for banana bread. Mash into a flat-bottomed bowl so you can press through the food until you feel the bottom of the bowl.

COOK

Mashed Potato Volcano

Serves 4 to 6

6 medium-size russet potatoes
1 1/4 cups milk
1 teaspoon salt
Red food coloring
3/4 cup shredded cheese of your choice, such
   as white cheddar, Monterey Jack, or
   other hard cheese

1. Preheat the oven to 450°F. Butter a pie or tart pan.
2. Peel the potatoes with a peeler and cut them into quarters. Bring a large pot of salted water to a boil and boil the potatoes for 20 minutes, until very tender. Drain.
3. In a large bowl, preferably with a flat bottom, mash the hot potatoes. Using an electric or rotary beater, beat the mashed potatoes, 3/4 cup of the milk, and the salt until fluffy. Set aside. (Beating the potatoes with the milk will make them fluffier, but if you wish, you can continue to use the masher for this step.)
4. To make the "lava," whisk together the remaining 1/2 cup milk with at least 10 drops of red food coloring. The more red you use, the "hotter" your lava will look. Mix in the shredded cheese.

PLAY
Mash Prints

Pour some acrylic paint onto a paper plate. Dip the masher into the paint and print designs on heavy paper. (Mashers have different patterns, so experiment with a variety.) For a variation, cut sponges into letters, geometric shapes, or anything you fancy and attach them to the bottom of your masher. (You can do this with a needle and thread or a twist tie poked through the sponges and secured to the masher's tines in several places.) Dip the sponge into the paint and mash prints onto the paper. Redip for each print. It's fun to experiment by applying different amounts of pressure to the masher.

5. Mound the mashed potatoes into the prepared pie pan, forming a volcano shape. Scoop out a hole in the middle; don't make it too deep, as you'll want the lava to bubble up and over the rim. Pour the lava mixture into the hole. You can use a fork or butter knife to create a few cracks and crevices along the rim and outside the volcano mound to help the lava's path. Bake for 15 minutes. Turn the oven to broil and, watching carefully, broil for a few minutes, until the top just starts to brown. Serve while hot and bubbly.

ROLLING PIN

Visions of Grandma—anyone's grandma—
tend to arise when you think of a rolling
pin. But give a kid a rolling pin, and that's
likely to change. Children love the rhythmic
feel and they like experimenting with how
much pressure to apply. To be successful
with a rolling pin, it's key for a child (or
anyone) to be high enough above the
work surface. Make sure that your
waist is no lower than the table-
or countertop in order to have
the strength and coordination
to roll out the dough.

PLAY (AND EAT)
Milk 'n' Cookie Crumbs

Rolling pins are good smashers for turning a bag full
of graham crackers or gingersnaps into chunky crumbs.
Place the cookies into a large zipper-lock plastic bag and
seal. With a toothpick, prick a small hole in the side of the
bag that's face up. This will allow just enough air to escape
but very few crumbs. Roll the rolling pin back and forth
over the bag of cookies until you've made crumbs. Turn the
bag 180 degrees now and then to ensure that all the cookies
crumble. Place the cookie crumbs into a shallow bowl. Dip a
clean finger into a cup of milk, then into the cookie crumbs.
Lick. Repeat.

COOK

Roll-Out Cookies

Makes 4 to 5 dozen cookies

1 cup (2 sticks) unsalted butter, softened
1 cup sugar
1 large egg
1 1/2 teaspoons vanilla extract
3 cups all-purpose flour
1 1/2 teaspoons baking powder
1/2 teaspoon salt
Royal Icing (page 15)
Food coloring

1. Place the butter and sugar together in a large bowl and, by hand or with an electric mixer, cream together until light and fluffy, about 2 minutes. Beat in the egg and vanilla extract until fully incorporated.

2. In another large bowl, stir together the flour, baking powder, and salt. Add the dry ingredients, 1/2 cup at a time, to the butter mixture, beating after each addition until just blended. (You can do this step by hand, but it is easier with an electric mixer.) Gather the dough and shape into several disks. Wrap each disk in plastic and chill in the refrigerator for at least 2 hours.

3. Preheat the oven to 350°F.

4. Using a floured rolling pin, roll out the dough on a lightly floured surface. Roll from the middle out in every direction until it is 1/4 to 1/2 inch thick. Cut out in shapes with cookie cutters and transfer to ungreased cookie sheets.

5. Bake for 8 to 10 minutes, until the cookies are light golden brown around the edges. Cool for 5 minutes on the cookie sheets before transferring the cookies to a wire rack to cool completely.

6. Ice with royal icing, let it dry, and paint with clean brushes dipped in slightly diluted food coloring.

COOK

Dog Bone Biscuits

Makes twenty-four 3 x 2-inch dog treats

2 cups whole-wheat flour
1 cup wheat germ or cornmeal
1 large egg
3 tablespoons vegetable oil
$\frac{1}{2}$ cup chicken broth
1 tablespoon minced fresh parsley
1 cup cooked leftover chicken, beef, or liver

1. Preheat the oven to 400°F. Lightly grease 2 baking sheets.
2. Combine the flour and wheat germ in a medium-size bowl.
3. In a large bowl, beat the egg with the vegetable oil. Beat in the broth. Add the dry ingredients to the egg mixture in batches, stirring well after each addition.
4. Put the parsley and meat in a food processor and chop finely. Fold the meat into the dough—preferably with your hands, as the dough will be very stiff. Turn the dough out onto a lightly floured surface and knead 10 times. Using a floured rolling pin, roll out the dough to a $\frac{1}{2}$ inch thickness. Cut into dog bone shapes with cookie cutters or by hand.
5. Place biscuits 1 inch apart on the prepared baking sheets. Bake for 20 minutes. Turn off the oven and let them air-dry inside for 6 hours or up to overnight. Store in an airtight container in the refrigerator for up to 2 weeks, or freeze for up to 3 months.

PLAY

Modern-Day Dioramas

Rolled-out clay, whether store-bought or homemade (page 60), makes an excellent platform for scene-based play using your own toys. Collect shoebox tops, shallow plastic containers, or anything else with a low lip. Roll out a large piece of clay with the rolling pin until it's somewhere between ½ and 1 inch thick. Gently set your box top on the clay to make sure you have a large enough piece of clay to cover the bottom. Transfer the clay to the inside of the box or container and press it into all the corners. Set the scene with small plastic people, animals, toys, play furniture—anything that will sink into the clay. The addition of toothpicks can be fun, too. These clay-based "sets" allow kids to change the players and dynamics. They're great for solo or play date fun.

ROTARY BEATER

Is any kitchen gadget more iconic than the rotary beater? It is a beautifully simple machine with transforming powers that delight and amaze children. Turn the crank, and heavy cream becomes butter! Egg whites grow into pointy mountain peaks! Most of us have electric beaters, but every now and then, especially when cooking with kids, it's nice to take the time to use this old-fashioned kitchen tool.

Peanut Butter and Jelly Pancakes

Makes 12 to 15 pancakes

1 cup all-purpose flour
2 tablespoons light brown sugar
2 teaspoons baking powder
$\frac{1}{2}$ cup smooth peanut butter
2 large eggs
1 $\frac{1}{4}$ cups whole or 2 percent milk
$\frac{1}{4}$ cup ($\frac{1}{2}$ stick) unsalted butter, melted
Jelly or jam in your favorite flavor

1. Combine the flour, brown sugar, and baking powder together in a medium-size bowl.
2. Place the peanut butter and eggs into a large bowl. Beat together with a rotary beater until the peanut butter is softened. Add the milk and melted butter and beat until well blended. Fold the dry ingredients into the wet ingredients with a rubber spatula.
3. Heat a griddle over medium-high heat. Pour the pancake batter onto the hot griddle, aiming to make each pancake 4 to 5 inches in diameter. Cook until bubbles pop and stay open, about

(continued on next page)

2 minutes, then flip and cook until the under-side is just browned. Transfer to a plate.

4. Spread a heaping teaspoon of jelly on half of the pancakes. Cover each with another pancake and serve sandwich-style. No syrup is required, and forks are optional!

What Else Can You Beat?

- **Turn heavy cream into whipped cream** by adding 2 tablespoons sugar for every 1 cup cream. Stop beating when you can form soft peaks.
- **Turn heavy cream into butter** by adding ½ teaspoon salt for every 1 cup cream. Beat until it clumps together like butter. Pour off any liquid that has accumulated in the bowl.
- **Beat egg whites until stiff.** If you come across a recipe that calls for stiff egg whites (such as a meringue recipe), get out the rotary beater. Kids find it very cool to watch the transparent liquid of egg whites transform into snow white peaks as they beat.

PLAY
Snow-Covered Candles

When you make "snow" out of hot, melted wax, you're perform-ing magic. You'll need to supervise this activity closely because of the hot wax, but kids can participate fully and will be delighted by the process and the results. These candles make great gifts for teachers and friends.

Adhesive tape
1 toothpick (or 1 for each candle)
1 large or several small cylinder-shaped candles
½ pound paraffin

Saucepan with a large metal bowl to fit on top
Plastic spoon
Sequins, beads, or tiny bells for decoration (optional)

1. Tape a toothpick to the wick of the candle, covering the wick completely with tape. This will protect it from the melted wax as you work.
2. Melt the paraffin in the metal bowl set over a saucepan of simmering water. Remove the bowl from the heat, set on a hotpad, and let it cool for about 60 seconds, or until you see wax just starting to set at the bottom of the bowl.
3. While you hold the bowl steady on the counter, your child can begin to beat the wax as fast as possible with the rotary beater. Take turns beating so you can keep up the speed. Wax will begin to increase in volume and turn into what looks like soap bubbles and then soft snow. Keep beating until you can't see any more liquidy melted wax.
4. Carefully roll the sides of the candles in the snowy wax. You can fill in any missed spots, as well as the top of your candle, with the back of a plastic spoon. While the wax remains warm and pliable, decorate by gently pushing sequins, beads, or other decorations into the wax, if you wish. When the candles have hardened (about 1 hour), remove the tape and toothpick.

> **CLEANING TIP** *To remove the wax from the metal bowl and the rotary beater, pour boiling water from a teakettle over them. The wax will melt right off.*

PLAY
Bowl of Bubbles

Set a large plastic mixing bowl in an empty sink or shallow pan. Add a few generous squirts of liquid dish soap to the bowl and add water to fill it halfway. Let your child beat away until the bubbles pile high above the bowl's rim. You can even beat until they overflow!

SALAD SPINNER

Push down on the pump, pull out the string, or crank the rotary handle, and you'll make this gadget spin and whir, and go very fast! Then you'll do it all over again.

COOK

Spinach Quesadillas

Serves 4

1 pound fresh spinach
1 tablespoon olive oil
1/3 cup sliced scallions (optional)
2 cloves garlic, minced
1 1/2 cups shredded cheese of your choice, such as mild cheddar or Monterey Jack, or other hard cheese
3/4 cup ricotta cheese
1/3 cup sour cream
Four 10-inch corn or whole-wheat tortillas

1. Soak the spinach in a large bowl of water; lift out gently, change the water, and soak again, until no grit remains in the bottom of the bowl. Spin dry in the salad spinner in batches, getting as much water as possible off the leaves. Set aside.
2. Heat the olive oil over medium heat in a pot large enough to hold all the spinach. Add the scallions, if using, and the garlic, cooking for a few minutes until soft but not brown. Add the spinach to the pot and cook for 3 minutes, stirring. Notice how much the spinach shrinks as it cooks!

3. Remove the pot from the heat and mix in the shredded cheese, ricotta cheese, and sour cream. Set aside.

4. In a large skillet over medium heat, warm the tortillas one at a time until flexible, about 15 seconds on each side. Spoon one-fourth of the spinach mixture onto one half of a tortilla. Fold the dry half over the spinach mixture to form a semicircle. Return the filled tortilla to the skillet and heat for 45 seconds. Flip the tortilla over and cook on the other side for 1 to 2 minutes. Transfer to an ovenproof plate, cover with aluminum foil, and keep warm in a 200°F oven while you prepare the other quesadillas.

PLAY
Spin Art

Cut out circles of drawing paper that will fit in the bottom of the salad spinner. Pour a few drops of food coloring (as many colors as you wish) or water-based tempera paint (thinned to the consistency of half-and-half) on the paper. Put the top on the spinner and let 'er rip! The action will spin the colors into a cool design on the paper.

SKEWERS

Don't ask me why, but kids love to eat off sticks. In my house, broccoli became palatable when it was skewered with alternating olives. And in this vein we have made "pops" from most food groups: cheese, fruit, bow tie pasta, cherry tomatoes, chicken, and more. Skewers made from bamboo also offer lots of possibilities when it comes to craft projects. I keep a tall glass filled with bamboo skewers on my kitchen shelf; they get used for food and fun all the time.

COOK

Dinner Kebabs

Children like to make kebabs as much as they like to eat them. Encourage little ones to make patterns. You can serve an entire meal in kebab form. Here are some ideas, but obviously you can substitute the foods your children love.

Sliced hot dogs and chunks of bun, with bowls of ketchup and mustard for dipping

Cherry tomatoes and cooked bow tie pasta, with a dip of olive oil mixed with Parmesan cheese

Chunks of sautéed chicken and olives, with a salsa dip

Cooked mini meatballs and cooked broad noodles, with a dip of marinara sauce

Cubes of cheddar cheese, sliced apples, and celery

Cooked baby carrots and steamed snow peas

Sliced bananas, strawberries, and melon, with a yogurt dip

Green and red grapes with Muenster cheese

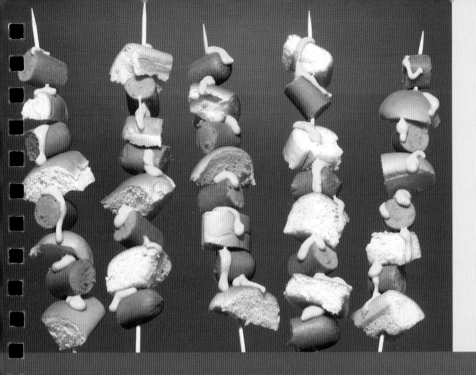

Experiment
Melted Gummi Banners

For this project, you will need two skewers and five gummi worms for each banner. Place five gummi worms onto a piece of parchment or waxed paper and heat in a microwave on high power for 20 seconds. Remove and let cool for 30 to 60 seconds. The melted candy should resemble a fruit roll-up. Peel the candy away from the paper, then roll each end around the end of a skewer. Gently pull the skewers apart to stretch the gummis into a banner. Experiment with different microwave heating times as well as different gummi colors.

SAFETY TIP *Don't serve hot dog chunks or mini meatballs to children under four, as they present a choking hazard.*

GADGET GUIDANCE *Once foods are skewered, it's nice to display them vertically. Good holders include apples, pumpkins, squash, and melons. A Styrofoam board will also work if you weigh it down.*

PLAY
Stick Figures

Puncture a cork with a bamboo skewer. Make a face on one side of the cork: Glue on small googly eyes; push a thumbtack in for a nose or draw one on with a marker; use a marker for the mouth too, or carve one into the cork. Glue colored yarn or crinkly paper onto the top of the cork to make hair. For arms and legs, get creative with paper, pipe cleaners, even doll clothing. Display your stick figures by sinking the flat ends of the skewers into more corks or lumps of clay.

SPATULA

The classic white rubber spatula has given way to a new generation made of silicone in a rainbow of colors that come in many shapes and sizes. They scrape batter from bowl to baking tin, or pudding from pot to serving dish. They are also excellent for licking.

COOK

Rainbow Cake

Serves 8 to 10

Nonstick cooking spray for the pan
1 cup all-purpose flour, plus more
    for dusting the pan
1 cup sugar
1 teaspoon baking powder
1/4 teaspoon salt
2/3 cup milk
1/4 cup (1/2 stick) butter, melted and cooled
1 large egg
1 1/4 teaspoons vanilla extract
1/2 cup colored nonpareils
2/3 cup vanilla frosting

1. Preheat the oven to 350°F. Spray an 8 x 8-inch baking pan with nonstick cooking spray, dust lightly with flour, and tap out the excess.
2. Combine the flour, sugar, baking powder, and salt in a large mixing bowl. Add the milk, butter, eggs, and vanilla extract. Using an electric mixer, beat for 3 minutes, until the batter is creamy. Set aside a heaping table-spoon of the nonpareils for the top of the cake and pour the rest into the batter. Fold them in with the spatula until well distributed. Pour the batter into the

prepared pan, scraping it all out of the bowl with the spatula.

3. Bake for 30 minutes, or until a toothpick or cake tester inserted into the middle comes out clean. Cool for 10 minutes in the pan, then invert, remove cake from pan, and cool completely on a rack.

4. Ice with the frosting and sprinkle the reserved nonpareils over the top.

PLAY
Baker's Clay

Stir it, pound it, make it, bake it! Use your spatula to whip up a batch of clay to bake and paint. Place ¾ cup warm water and ½ cup salt in a large bowl. Stir with the spatula until the salt begins to dissolve. Add 2 cups flour and stir again until you form a ball. Knead it for 5 to 10 minutes, until the dough is smooth. Add a tiny bit of water if the dough is too dry, or flour if it's too sticky. Little kids who like to pound will enjoy using the flat end of the spatula to smack down lumps of the dough and get them as flat as possible. Or they can "cut" the dough into pieces with the spatula and shape it as desired. Once you have formed shapes, bake the clay at 300°F for 45 minutes to 1 hour. Let cool completely and then paint with tempera paints.

SPREADER

Spreaders are little knives with blades dull enough to be safe but perfectly effective in cutting bananas, avocados, and other soft things. Their small, short handles fit well in little hands, and when kids use them "by myself" it strengthens confidence and independence.

Experiment
Marbleizing

How do you make a marbled pattern? Try adding melted chocolate to vanilla pudding, chocolate batter to vanilla batter, or jam to slightly warmed Marshmallow Fluff. Gently push a spreader through the mixture, as if you're cutting right through the liquid. Try swirling the spreader or making lines in one direction and then the other. It's fun to experiment with patterns.

Fruit Salad, Jr.

Serves 3

1 banana, peeled
6 strawberries, hulled
1 peach, plum, or nectarine
1/4 cantaloupe or honeydew melon
1 cup vanilla yogurt (optional)
Novelty toothpicks (optional)

1. Place the banana on a cutting board, preferably one with rubber feet so it doesn't move. Show your child how to press the spreader gently through the fruit to cut off a bite-size piece. Place each cut piece (that isn't eaten first!) into a medium-size mixing bowl.
2. Cut the strawberries into quarters with the spreader and add them to the bowl.
3. Cut the rest of the fruit into flat-sided pieces before your child slices them with the spreader and adds them to the bowl.
4. Toss the fruit together gently and top with the yogurt, if desired. Or skip the yogurt and serve the fruit salad with whimsical toothpicks.

PLAY
Clay Chop

Roll store-bought Play-Doh or Easy Homemade Play Clay (page 60) into colored logs. Use the spreader to "chop" into "firewood." The more logs you roll, the more firewood you can chop. Try stacking the logs in matchbox containers. Or instead of logs, can you make a long papa snake and some teeny tiny baby snakes?

GADGET GUIDANCE *When measuring teaspoons of baking powder or baking soda or cups of flour for a recipe, a spreader is a good tool to scrape off the excess for that perfect measurement. Older kids like this job; call them in when you're mixing dry ingredients together.*

TEA BALL

A tea ball is fun because it traps stuff inside—tea leaves, plastic spiders, tiny rubber balls. Your child is in charge of what goes in and when it comes out, a powerful proposition for a little kid. Because it acts as an infuser, you can have fun experimenting with drinkable concoctions. And because it's a strainer, it makes a great addition to a collection of bath toys.

COOK

Hot Cider with Swizzle Sticks

Serves 8 to 10

8 cups apple cider
1/2 cup packed light brown sugar
One 3-inch cinnamon stick, broken into pieces
1 teaspoon whole allspice
1 teaspoon whole cloves

Small piece of whole nutmeg (optional), smashed
with a hammer or meat pounder
Flavored candy swizzle sticks

1. Combine the cider and brown sugar in a large saucepan. Place the cinnamon, allspice, cloves, and nutmeg into a tea ball and add to the cider. Bring to a boil, reduce the heat, and simmer for 20 minutes.
2. Remove the tea ball, pour the cider into mugs, and serve warm with a candy swizzle stick.

PLAY
Drinkable Magic Potion

Empty the leaves from 3 berry-flavored tea bags (Celestial Seasonings Wild Berry Zinger works well) into the tea ball. Put the ball into a bowl and pour in 2 cups warm to hot water. Swish or stir it until the water turns an appealing shade of red. Continue stirring and recite some magic words. Pour into glasses and add a pinch of wizard or fairy dust (colored or sanding sugar is perfect). Drink up and watch your secret powers emerge!

Experiment
ExperiMint

Make a minty drink by adding fresh peppermint or spearmint leaves to a tea ball. Add boiling water and infuse for 5 to 10 minutes. Let cool until it's not too hot to sip. What can you add to sweeten? Try maple syrup, sugar cubes, or honey, and decide which you like best.

TONGS

Tongs make it easy to dip and flip foods, as well as to move things from one place to another. They come in many sizes and materials and are handy for foods as diverse as sugar cubes, ice, salad, steak, and escargots! Kids can use any type of tongs, although the spring-loaded kind are the easiest to manipulate.

COOK

Chocolate-Covered Frozen Banana Pops

Serves 6

3 ripe bananas
9 ounces semisweet chocolate
2 ounces whole milk or cream
3 teaspoons vegetable oil

Topping choices:
    Rainbow sprinkles
    Shredded coconut
    Chopped nuts

6 lollipop or craft sticks

1. Line a baking sheet with parchment or waxed paper and set aside.
2. Peel the bananas. With a spreader or knife, cut them in half horizontally.

3. Melt the chocolate together with the milk and vegetable oil in a metal bowl set over a saucepan of simmering water or in a microwave-safe dish. Stir until blended.

4. Choose your toppings and pour them onto individual small plates. With the tongs, drop the banana pieces one by one into the melted chocolate. When completely coated, lift the bananas out with the tongs and place them on the plate with the desired topping. Use tongs or fingers to roll the banana in the topping to coat it. Place finished bananas on the prepared baking sheet.

5. Insert lollipop sticks into the flat end of each banana and place the baking sheet in the freezer. Freeze for 1 hour, then eat or wrap each banana pop in plastic and store in the freezer for up to 1 week.

PLAY
Two-Team Tong Race

Make your starting line a table or bench. Put pairs of any of the following objects out on the table (one object for each person or team): Ping-Pong ball, paper clip, cooked spaghetti, sugar cube, bowl of ice cubes, toothbrush, pen, gummi worm, sock, capped marker, pretzel, baby carrot, piece of paper, old stuffed animal. The object of the game is to pick up each item from the table with a pair of tongs and deposit it in a bucket on the other side of the room or yard. No hands can touch the objects! If something falls, you must pick it up with the tongs. The team that fills its bucket first wins.

WHISK

The balloon-shaped wires of a whisk make it a cool-looking gadget, and it's light enough for children to easily handle. Scientifically it's interesting because by whisking a liquid (heavy cream, say) you are essentially adding lots of air to it, expanding the volume. The trick of the whisk is in the wrist action. To practice good whisking technique, hold the tool in the air and make little circles. When you dip the whisk into a bowl of liquid, keep that circular motion (not stirring) going. Think of it more as folding than stirring, and you will soon get the hang of using a whisk.

84

COOK

Open-Faced Omelet

Serves 4

1 tablespoon olive oil
3 tablespoons chopped onion
1 clove garlic, sliced
1 large baking potato, peeled and diced
6 large eggs
2 tablespoons water
1/4 teaspoon salt
1 tablespoon butter
3 tablespoons shredded cheddar cheese
3 slices bacon, cooked and crumbled

1. Heat the olive oil in a medium-size sauté pan. Add the onion and garlic and cook, stirring, for 1 minute, until the garlic just starts to brown. Add the potato cubes and cook, stirring occasionally, until they are soft, about 20 minutes. Set aside.
2. Preheat the broiler with the top oven rack placed closest to the heat.
3. Break the eggs into a medium-size mixing bowl. Add the water and salt. Whisk briskly

until well blended. (Counting to 100 while whisking will make for a light, puffy omelet.)

4. In a large sauté pan with an ovenproof handle, melt the butter over medium-low heat. Pour the eggs into the pan. Swirl to make sure the eggs cover the bottom of the pan and cook for 1 minute.

5. Gently spoon the potato mixture over the eggs. Top potatoes with the cheese and bacon. Transfer the pan to the broiler to finish cooking the top of the omelet, about 2 minutes. Keep your eye on it, as it will be done when the eggs puff up and the cheese is golden brown and bubbly.

Experiment
Aromatic Potpourri

Potpourri is a mixture of dried flowers, leaves, herbs, and spices that is placed in open containers, such as small boxes or bowls, to scent a room. There are no set ingredients for potpourri, so it is fun to explore a variety of aromas. A whisk is a great tool for drying flowers to get you started.

To dry petals, gather fresh flowers that are in full bloom but not yet turning brown. Vary the length of the stems. Hang a large whisk upside down in a spot without much light. Thread flower stems through the wires of the whisk, letting the petals hang in the air to dry. Keep layering upward, varying the stem lengths to keep petals from touching. You may need to attach a light weight to some of the stems to hold them horizontally (try a piece of string taped to a dime). The flowers are ready when the petals are crisp and dry, usually after about 1 week.

Let kids personalize their batches by choosing among lemon, lime, and orange rinds. Set several spices out in small bowls so kids can choose their favorites. Turn the page for some other creative suggestions for your potpourri.

For each cup of petals, add any of the following:

- ¼ cup dried aromatic leaves, such as mint or eucalyptus
- ¼ cup dried herbs, such as thyme, rosemary, chamomile, or lavender
- Spices, such as broken cinnamon sticks or whole cloves
- Bits of dried citrus rind
- Dried miniature pinecones, berries, or thin wood chips
- ¼ teaspoon orrisroot powder (a fixative, available where spices or gardening supplies are sold)
- Several drops of essential oil in any aroma you like

Mix everything gently together with your hands. Place the mixture in a brown paper bag lined with waxed paper. Fold and seal the bag with a paper clip and leave in a dry, dark, cool place for 2 weeks. Shake the bag gently from time to time to blend the scents. Place your homemade potpourri in open containers around your house.

PLAY
Whisk Maracas

Gently insert several jingle bells between the wires of a balloon-shaped whisk. Instant instrument! Add colored pompons to change the sound. Bells can be purchased from craft supply stores and come in a variety of sizes. The small ones will work at the bottom of the whisk where the wires are closely spaced. Use bigger bells at the top.

RESOURCE GUIDE

Amazon.com
www.amazon.com
Amazon has a remarkably robust kitchen store; you can browse by brand or by category. Check out the great collection of nesting bowls.

Apple Source
1716 Apples Road
Chapin, IL 62628
Phone: (800) 588-3854
Fax: (217) 245-7844
www.applesource.com
This site sells the original Back to Basics Apple Peeler, as well as corers, food mills, and several other tools. It offers lots of nifty apple facts, too.

Crate and Barrel
1250 Techny Road
Northbrook, IL 60062
Phone: (800) 967-6696
www.crateandbarrel.com
Crate and Barrel's "gadget bins" are always filled with useful, well-priced cooking tools. Whether shopping in a store, online, or by catalog, you'll find kitchenware in wonderful colors that really appeal to kids. Buy the spatulas that match the nesting bowls that match the citrus squeezer!

The Gadget Source
Calvert Retail, LP
P.O. Box 302
Montchanin, DE 19710
Phone: (800) 458-2616
Fax: (302) 622-8602
www.thegadgetsource.com
The Gadget Source carries cooking tools, and cooking tools only, so the staff really knows its gadgets. Look for a large and always interesting selection of new and classic tools. Sometimes this site stocks unusual items, such as a finger-sandwich cutter or a potato peeler for lefties. A catalog is also available.

Good Dog Express
909 Admore Drive
Kent, OH 44240
Phone: (877) 682-7387
www.gooddogexpress.com
An amusing and surprisingly large collection of dog bone–shaped cookie cutters (and cake pans, too) are available at this online store.

Kitchen Collectables, Inc.
8901 J Street, Suite 2
Omaha, NE 68127
Phone: (888) 593-2436
Fax: (402) 593-1151
www.kitchengifts.com
This site is my favorite for cookie cutters: Imagine a magic wand, a little red wagon, or any of the 50 states. If you can't find what you're looking for among the selection of 2,500 cookie cutters, you can order one that's custom-made. Kitchen Collectables carries meringue powder (an ingredient for royal icing) and a good selection of kitchen gadgets, too.

MoMA Design and Book Store
11 West 53rd Street
New York, NY 10019
Phone: (800) 447-6662
www.momastore.org
If you're looking for gadgets with both style and design, you'll be hard-pressed to find a nicer selection than the one at New York's Museum of Modern Art. It carries cool (if sometimes pricey) kitchenware, such as brightly colored cutting boards and collapsible colanders and funnels from all over the world. Parents will appreciate the innovative designs.

Old Will Knott Scales
1738 S Van Buren Street
Enid, OK 73703
Phone: (866) 867-5400
www.oldwillknott.com
Old Will Knott sells scales for every kind of use—including the kitchen. The Web site is fun to browse with kids, as you can see an amazing selection of balancing instruments, from talking digital scales to old-fashioned balance scales.

OXO International
75 Ninth Avenue
New York, NY 10011
Phone: (800) 545-4411
www.oxo.com
Though Oxo products are sold in many kitchenware stores, you can also go right to the source online. Their rubber-handled tools help kids get an easy, comfortable grip.

Sur La Table
5701 Sixth Avenue South, Suite 486
Seattle, WA 98108
Phone: (800) 243-0852
Fax: (206) 613-6137
www.surlatable.com
Sur La Table is a nationwide kitchen store with a solid gadget selection, beautiful children's aprons, and whimsical items with kid appeal, such as animal-shaped egg cups and ice cream scoops. Look for fun stuff at holiday time, like Easter egg spatulas or heart-shaped bowls.

United States Plastic Corporation
1390 Neubrecht Road
Lima, OH 45801
Phone: (800) 809-4217
Fax: (800) 854-5498
www.usplastic.com
This is not a cooking site, although it has plenty of kitchen gadgets in its vast inventory. Hands down, it has the largest and most interesting selection of funnels, starting at prices under a dollar.

Williams-Sonoma
3250 Van Ness Avenue
San Francisco, CA 94109
Phone: (877) 812-6235
www.williams-sonoma.com
At Williams-Sonoma, you can buy everything for your kitchen, from measuring spoons to molten chocolate cake batter! It stocks some clever gadgets that are Williams-Sonoma exclusives. You can shop by Web, store, or catalog.

Wilton Industries
2240 West 75th Street
Woodbridge, IL 60517
Phone: (800) 794-5866
www.wilton.com
Wilton is a baker's heaven. It carries absolutely everything for baking, including character-shaped pans, hundreds of colored and sanding sugars, cake decorations, cupcake liners, lollipop sticks, and pastry bags and tips. Kids like perusing the catalog and Web site as much as adults do.

MEASUREMENT EQUIVALENTS

Please note that all conversions are approximate.

LIQUID CONVERSIONS

U.S.	Metric
1 tsp	5 ml
1 tbs	15 ml
2 tbs	30 ml
3 tbs	45 ml
¼ cup	60 ml
⅓ cup	75 ml
⅓ cup + 1 tbs	90 ml
⅓ cup + 2 tbs	100 ml
½ cup	120 ml
⅔ cup	150 ml
¾ cup	180 ml
¾ cup + 2 tbs	200 ml
1 cup	240 ml
1 cup + 2 tbs	275 ml
1 ¼ cups	300 ml
1 ⅓ cups	325 ml
1 ½ cups	350 ml
1 ⅔ cups	375 ml
1 ¾ cups	400 ml
1 ¾ cups + 2 tbs	450 ml
2 cups (1 pint)	475 ml
2 ½ cups	600 ml
3 cups	720 ml
4 cups (1 quart)	945 ml (1,000 ml is 1 liter)

WEIGHT CONVERSIONS

U.S./U.K.	Metric
½ oz	14 g
1 oz	28 g
1 ½ oz	43 g
2 oz	57 g
2 ½ oz	71 g
3 oz	85 g
3 ½ oz	100 g
4 oz	113 g
5 oz	142 g
6 oz	170 g
7 oz	200 g
8 oz	227 g
9 oz	255 g
10 oz	284 g
11 oz	312 g
12 oz	340 g
13 oz	368 g
14 oz	400 g
15 oz	425 g
1 lb	454 g

OVEN TEMPERATURE CONVERSIONS

°F	Gas Mark	°C
250	½	120
275	1	140
300	2	150
325	3	165
350	4	180
375	5	190
400	6	200
425	7	220
450	8	230
475	9	240
500	0	260
5500	Broil	290

INDEX